Queen Elizabeth II

Queen
Elizabeth II
The British Monarchy Today

Douglas Liversidge

Arthur Barker Limited
London

A subsidiary of Weidenfeld (Publishers) Ltd.

Acknowledgement is made to Cassell & Co. Ltd.
for permission to publish extracts from *The Crown
and the People* by HRH the Duke of Windsor.

ISBN 0 213 16495 7

Printed in Great Britain by
Willmer Brothers Limited, Birkenhead

Contents

ॐ Illustrations

The illustration on the front of the jacket showing Queen Elizabeth at the State Opening of Parliament is reproduced by permission of Fox Photos.

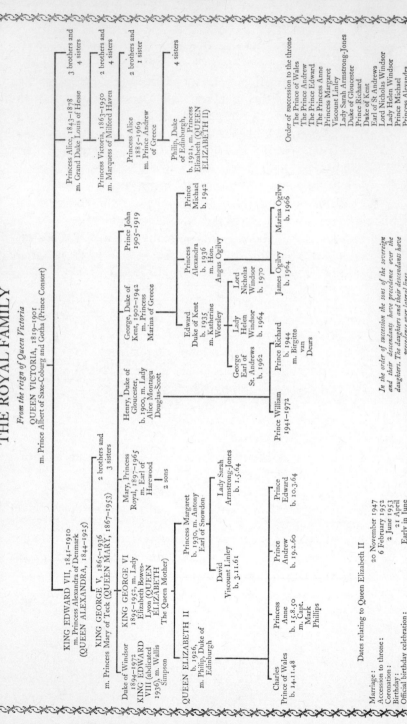

THE ROYAL FAMILY

From the reign of Queen Victoria

QUEEN VICTORIA, 1819–1901
m. Prince Albert of Saxe-Coburg and Gotha (Prince Consort)

KING EDWARD VII, 1841–1910
m. Princess Alexandra of Denmark
(QUEEN ALEXANDRA, 1844–1925)

KING GEORGE V, 1865–1936
m. Princess Mary of Teck (QUEEN MARY, 1867–1953)

Duke of Windsor 1894–1972 KING EDWARD VIII (abdicated 1936), m. Wallis Simpson

KING GEORGE VI 1895–1952, m. Lady Elizabeth Bowes-Lyon (QUEEN ELIZABETH The Queen Mother)

Mary, Princess Royal, 1897–1965, m. Earl of Harewood
2 sons

2 brothers and 3 sisters

Henry, Duke of Gloucester, b. 1900, m. Lady Alice Montagu Douglas-Scott

George, Duke of Kent, 1902–1942 m. Princess Marina of Greece

Prince John 1905–1919

Princess Alice, 1843–1878
m. Grand Duke Louis of Hesse
3 brothers and 4 sisters

Princess Victoria, 1863–1950
m. Marquess of Milford Haven
2 brothers and 4 sisters

Princess Alice 1885–1969 m. Prince Andrew of Greece
2 brothers and 1 sister

Philip, Duke of Edinburgh, b. 1921, m. Princess Elizabeth (QUEEN ELIZABETH II)
4 sisters

QUEEN ELIZABETH II b. 1926, m. Philip, Duke of Edinburgh

Princess Margaret b. 1930, m. Antony Earl of Snowdon

David Viscount Linley b. 3.11.61

Lady Sarah Armstrong-Jones b. 1.5.64

Charles Prince of Wales b. 14.11.48

Princess Anne b. 15.8.50 m. Capt. Mark Phillips

Prince Andrew b. 19.2.60

Prince Edward b. 10.3.64

Prince William 1941–1972

George Earl of St Andrews b. 1962

Edward Duke of Kent b. 1935 m. Katherine Worsley

Lady Helen Windsor b. 1964

Prince Richard b. 1944 m. Birgitte van Deurs

Princess Alexandra b. 1936 m. Hon. Angus Ogilvy

Lord Nicholas Windsor b. 1970

Prince Michael b. 1942

James Ogilvy b. 1964

Marina Ogilvy b. 1966

Order of succession to the throne
The Prince of Wales
The Prince Andrew
The Prince Edward
The Princess Anne
Princess Margaret
Viscount Linley
Lady Sarah Armstrong-Jones
Duke of Gloucester
Prince Richard
Duke of Kent
Earl of St Andrews
Lord Nicholas Windsor
Lady Helen Windsor
Prince Michael
Princess Alexandra

In the order of succession the sons of the sovereign and their descendants have precedence over the daughters. The daughters and their descendants have precedence over lateral lines.

Dates relating to Queen Elizabeth II

Marriage :   20 November 1947
Accession to throne :   6 February 1952
Coronation :   2 June 1953
Birthday :   21 April
Official birthday celebration :   Early in June

ஃ 1 *Scenes of Childhood*

In the fitful spring of 1926 – a time of acute industrial strife in Britain – Sir William Joynson-Hicks, Home Secretary in Baldwin's second Government, answered a summons to a house in London's Mayfair. A royal baby was about to be born, an event which in those days demanded the Minister's presence. This antiquated custom harked back to a bitter wrangle over another birth when Mary of Modena, wife of the maligned Roman Catholic James II and thought to be incapable of child bearing, had in July 1688 surprisingly delivered a son. Horrified by the prospect of yet another Papist on the throne, the Protestant Whigs had furiously denounced the offspring as some low-born infant smuggled into the Queen's bedchamber in a warming pan. Even to the most bigoted, this 'plot' was hardly credible. Yet from it emerged the practice – a quaint anachronism by the twentieth century – for someone responsible to Parliament to guarantee the legitimate claims of anyone who might some day wear the Crown.

Thus, in an hour-long vigil, Sir William stoutly safeguarded the realm from Jacobite or other nefarious intrigue. A baby girl came into the world and yawned lazily at Sir William, who briskly announced to the nation: 'Her Royal Highness the Duchess of York was safely delivered of a princess at 2.40 A.M. this morning, Wednesday, April 21st.'

At Windsor Castle the reigning monarch King George V and Queen Mary were awakened and given the news. 'Such a relief and joy', recorded the jubilant Queen in her diary. Could she have peered into the distant future her next entry would have foretold further happiness, for among the guests who stayed to luncheon that same day was Princess Andrew of Greece. Twenty-one years hence Philip, her four-year-old son, would become the husband of the baby girl in the rooftop nursery which overlooked a gallimaufry of Mayfair chimney pots and mews.

To his brother the Prince of Wales, then recuperating in Biarritz, the Duke sent a telegram happily announcing the birth. In those more carefree days, the heir apparent was unaware that when his little niece was ten years old he would be the principal in an unprecedented crisis that would dramatically threaten the throne. For him the outcome would be the loneliness of exile; for her the unexpected path to queenship.

But even at the moment of the child's birth Britain by no means lacked harassment, yet in a quite different sense. Indeed the Yorks' first child had arrived like a ray of sun on a dismal national scene, piercing leaden skies of social discontent. For the moment not even the cold, spiteful rain could dampen the joy of the people. (From the novelist Arnold Bennett, who had lately become the father of an illegitimate child, we learn that the 'weather has been foul for a week'.)

And so the guns roared their greeting from the Tower of London and in Hyde Park, and, conveying the emotions of the nation as well as speculating on things to come, the *Daily Mail* observed: 'The baby who was the chief topic of conversation throughout the kingdom yesterday could conceivably become Queen of England.'

But soon there were other and critical matters to comment upon: a grave calamity which would long leave Britain scarred. On 3 May – thirteen days after the birth of the future Queen Elizabeth II – the country plunged deeply into the frightful chaos of the General Strike. For ten days an enfeebled nation was convulsed and then virtually paralysed by its impact. And, even when the General Council of the Trades Union Congress capitulated, the miners, with the traditional stubborness of their hardy breed, refused to surrender; sullen and embittered, not until November did they admit defeat. Meanwhile the output of coal, on which British industry was then so desperately reliant, was nil, a factor which imperilled the national economy.

It was a sombre birthright for a little Princess destined to wear the Crown twenty-six years hence, reigning over a nation wounded by the social clash which has still not been resolved.

All this, however, was an ominous symptom of the times, not only in Britain but throughout the West at large. The inspiring patriotic spirit which had borne the British along despite the perils and adversities of the First World War had been replaced by cynicism and despair. As Prime Minister, Lloyd George had volubly predicted 'a country fit for heroes', but now, to the lean-faced on the hunger marches, Welsh oratory rang with a derisive hollowness. In the trail of a postwar boom had slunk the tragedies and harsh realities of a slump. Forced into stark poverty the defeated countries had been too poor to buy. Finally the world's economy wilted and nations crashed. They were hard, exacting times for all, but much worse for some. Unemployment ran amok in the wake of depression and ushered in the dole. It was the sterile period of *The Hollow Men* and *The Waste Land*, in which T. S. Eliot graphically portrayed the miseries of class disunion.

Yet in actual fact it was part of the social revolution which, stirring first in the years of the genial, gregarious Edward VII, was to gather momentum in each successive reign. There would be no signs of its abatement even in the years of Queen Elizabeth II.

The major key to social change was the grim struggle of the Socialist movement. Six months before the Duchess of York's own birth in 1900, the British Labour Party had rented its first offices, occupying rooms in Farringdon Street in the City of London. The emergence of Socialism as a third great faction would give a new and significant dimension to the British political scene. The power that for centuries had been the prerogative of the aristocracy and the influential well-to-do was slowly but relentlessly being grasped by the working-class millions and their leaders.

It was a situation which roused pronounced misgivings and

uneasiness at Court. Memories of the postwar revolution which had brutally overtaken ancient dynasties were still too freshly etched in the mind for complacency. In February 1924, some two years before the future Elizabeth II was born, King George V (Grandpa England as his little granddaughter would eventually call him) received with some alarm the news of the fall of Baldwin's Conservative Government. In Britain Socialism had arrived at last and the moderate-minded King, in spite of persistent qualms, had no alternative but to deal with it. Rigidly conforming to constitutional duty, he somewhat reluctantly invited Ramsay MacDonald to form Britain's first Labour administration.

The late Duke of Windsor, recording the sole authentic account of his father's initial encounter with his new Labour Ministers, wrote in his book *Crown and People*:

They included, besides Ramsay MacDonald, who had begun his career as a low-paid clerk, three trade unionists – the colourful J. H. Thomas, who had been an engine driver; Arthur Henderson, who had been a foundry labourer; and J. R. Clynes, who had been a millhand.

My father had been shocked by a report that his new Prime Minister had presided over a public meeting at the Albert Hall only shortly before, at which the Bolshevik anthem, the Internationale, had been enthusiastically sung. Fixing Ramsay MacDonald with a cold eye to show his concern and disapproval, the King asked squarely whether the newspaper accounts of this incident were true. The Prime Minister admitted with some embarrassment that the song had indeed been sung that evening. 'But that is a dreadful thing to do,' said the King. Ramsay MacDonald agreed but added, to my father's consternation, that his followers would in fact have sung it again in the House of Commons in jubilation over the defeat of the Conservatives but for his restraining influence and that of his moderate colleagues.

'Good Lord', exclaimed the King, 'they'll sing it outside

the Palace next'. Shamefacedly, the Prime Minister exclaimed, 'The trouble is, your Majesty, that they have lately got used to singing that song and it may take a little time to break them of this habit.'

That evening my father recorded in his diary, "Today twenty-three years ago dear Grandma died. I wonder what she would have thought of a Labour Government.'

George v was distressed by the class strife that 'introduced new and unfamiliar violences in British life'. But the quickening tempo of social change would be so pronounced that, by the time his granddaughter sat on the throne, the Internationale would itself be an anachronism in Britain. She would invite the Labour leaders of the day to form administrations without the slightest risk of undermining the throne. Yet Grandpa England – the monarch who was unmistakably conservative in outlook, treating innovation with marked distrust and sincerely loathing class war in all its forms – was largely instrumental in effecting that harmony. Reactionary he may have been, yet it was precisely his unquestionable concern for all his subjects – plus the strict concept of his duties as a constitutional monarch – that gave stability to both Crown and people, a stability which has reached its zenith in the reign of Elizabeth II. Indeed it can be argued with cogency that the most stabilizing element in Britain is the royal family. Its political impartiality and commendable standards of morality give the right ballast to the ship of state.

Change during this century, both technical and social, was clearly inevitable. There was scope for change even in the royal family itself. Not long before, Albert, Duke of York, could never have married Lady Elizabeth Bowes-Lyon for she was a commoner; inflexible royal etiquette would have been an unsurmountable obstruction. The unyielding, overpowering Hanoverian practice debarred such unions, persisting up to the marriage of King George v (then also Duke of York) and Princess Mary of Teck. Victoria, the Queen Empress, had crystallized this absurdity with the words: 'A morganatic marriage is something we would *never* wish to discuss'.

But even in her own eventful lifetime Victoria – known as the 'Grandmother of Europe' because of her close family relationships with other royal dynasties – was to appreciate the folly of this rigorous rule. Europe's royal hierarchy was dominated by the Habsburgs, Hohenzollerns, Coburgs and Romanovs: socially a rarefied set, but intermarriage within this exclusive circle had taken its sinister toll in the form of the fearful blood disease of haemophilia. Painful to her memory, this 'scourge of Kings' would destroy even Victoria's own son, Leopold, as well as grandchildren and great-grandchildren. And because this horror was traceable to the females of these ancient lineages it was time to inject new blood by broadening the sphere of marriage.

Even so it had been customary for the sons of Britain's reigning family to choose their brides from among the daughters of Europe's old nobility. But Albert, Duke of York (known as Bertie in the royal family) brought about a drastic change. His choice of bride was, as *The Times* commented, 'Truly British to the core!' Moreover it caused the timely death of a tradition whereby royal betrothals were influenced by political and dynastic alliances – a system which itself was grossly out of step with modern times. Not that Elizabeth Bowes-Lyon, ninth child of the Earl and Countess of Strathmore and Kinghorne, need hesitate to compare her genealogy with that of the foremost noble houses of Europe or, for that matter, the House of Windsor to which her husband belonged. Glamis Castle, the ancestral Scottish fortress, had passed down in an unbroken line for almost six centuries. In this respect even the royal family was outshone.

It is imperative to fathom the ancestry and upbringing of 'the little Duchess', for therein lies the key to her endearing and remarkable character which was to have such a decisive influence on her daughter Queen Elizabeth II. Indeed her striking qualities, as will be seen later, were to have enormous impact on two future monarchs – her husband as well as her elder daughter. Curiously, although a commoner (because she is not of the blood royal), she can trace her impressive lineage to remote Scottish kings. And by a remarkable coincidence Robert II, the first of the Stuart sovereigns, was an ancestor common to both herself and her husband.

The noble family of Bowes-Lyon began with the adventurous Sir John Lyon of Forteviot, who in 1376 married Lady Jean Stuart, Robert's widowed daughter, whose dower was the castellated Glamis Castle. Although the Duchess's father was a Stuart Scot, as a young cavalry officer he had turned (like his predecessors) to England when taking a wife. In his case the Englishwoman was Nina Cecilia Cavendish-Bentinck, the daughter of a minister of religion and the cousin of the sixth Duke of Portland. An outstanding person by any standards, she could trace her ancestry not merely to Dutch aristocrats who accompanied William of Orange to England in 1688 but also to the union of the Lancastrian Henry VII and Elizabeth of York.

Of an intensely practical nature and skilled in household affairs, Lady Strathmore instilled in her children the need for efficiency in the domestic arts. To the Countess cookery, sewing and house management were more rewarding than mathematics. That was the educational pattern, then, of the future Duchess of York. Nor was money lavished upon her. Indeed, viewed in the light of their lofty niche in society, the Strathmores were by no means rich. As a child the Duchess assisted in conducting tourists around Glamis and tips were never declined. Sometimes in her youth cash was so lamentably scarce that she patiently queued with friends for the cheaper seats at London theatres. One day she would recall personal experiences when teaching her own daughters the meaning of thrift, restricting them to one shilling per week.

Most important of all, as Hector Bolitho, her biographer, had written, Elizabeth Bowes-Lyon 'grew up in an atmosphere of good talk, music and all the accomplishments of an intelligent family'. This formula, based on good sense, she would apply to the child who would in due course be Queen Elizabeth II.

Basically the Strathmores were simple country folk, devoting

7

B

their energies to their Scottish and English estates and the many people who faithfully served them. None sought eminence in the exalted affairs of state, although the Earl often attended debates in the House of Lords. At such times the family would move to London, to their town house, then in St James's Square, or to their Queen Anne mansion, St Paul's, Waldenbury, a rural pleasance in Hertfordshire. But the Strathmores were well known at Court. Indeed, during the months that the royal family temporarily left London for Balmoral, the Bowes-Lyons never failed to reside at Glamis, only some thirty miles away.

By all accounts it was in London, at a party given by the Countess of Leicester at Montague House, that Elizabeth and Bertie first met. She was five years old and he was nine. Gossip claims that, typical of her innate kindness, she gave him the crystallized cherries from her sugar cake.

But the story of Elizabeth II really began on a resplendent January afternoon in 1923 when the young Duke of York drove through the wintry Hertfordshire countryside to the Strathmores' English house. Ostensibly he was attending a house party but his mission was in reality to seek the Lady Elizabeth's hand. The day was the thirteenth of the month and to the superstitious might have augured failure. But the Prince refused to be deterred. Despite his acute nervousness and the lack of encouragement which almost seemed to amount to indifference, he had already been a persistent suitor for the past two years. His parents had long been aware of his deep regard, but George V had told him with characteristic bluffness: 'You will be very lucky if she has you.'

The next day, as the couple wandered through a woodland haunt of Elizabeth's childhood, Bertie mustered the courage to propose. It is said, however, that the agonizing stammer that always tormented him left him speechless; he therefore wrote the proposal in a notebook, and to his delight was readily accepted. Some years after her marriage Elizabeth confided to a friend: 'It was my duty to marry Bertie and I fell in love with him afterwards.' To Queen Mary, then at Sandringham, the ex-sailor wired joyfully: 'All right. Bertie'. In a subsequent letter he said, 'I am very, very happy, and I can only hope that Elizabeth feels the same as I do. I know I am very lucky to have won her over at last.'

At that precise moment Bertie did not realize how incisively history would echo his sentiments. The quiet strength of character and the captivating charm of 'the smiling Duchess' would be significant in the destiny of the throne. Temporarily the Crown would tarnish, but she would help to save it, thus ensuring the reign of her daughter Elizabeth. Resilient and cool, her influence would be far reaching, both as the wife of a king and the mother of a queen.

Congratulating the Duke on his choice of fiancée, *The Times* commented: 'There is one wedding to which the people look forward with still deeper interest – the wedding which will give a wife to the Heir to the Throne. . . .' So far Bertie's elder brother the Prince of Wales had shown no inclination towards marriage, but when eventually he did contemplate matrimony it would cause deeper anguish than interest for many.

As invariably happens on royal occasions, the engagement and the subsequent marriage at Westminster Abbey on the following 23 April temporarily occupied the people's minds, helping for the moment to mitigate the fears of social conflict and international strife which pressed heavily. Britain was passing through a phase of terrible depression, and in Europe jackboots marching in the Ruhr sounded like an evil omen of the tragedy to come. But for a while the people's eyes were focused on the royal family and a keenly debated topic occupied their minds. In the abbey there had been no wedding of a royal Prince since Richard II some five centuries earlier. The forthcoming marriage therefore seemed to merit some unique treatment. Why not broadcast the event, enthused the progressives. The technique of wireless telephony, as it was then called, had reached a pitch whereby programmes could now be heard in most parts of Britain. Yet there were reactionaries who opposed this latest contribution from science. Perversely defying all rational argument the Dean and Chapter were unshakable in their contention that the new medium would shatter the reverence of the marriage rite. Ironically the day would dawn when the Church hierarchy would greet not only radio in cathedral and church but also the brassier medium of television. As for monarchy, both media would figure among the greatest assets of the royal family, binding it more closely with the people, especially during the reign of Elizabeth II.

Meanwhile in Westminster Abbey, that venerable shrine of the Kings and Queens of England, the Yorks were married. In addressing the bride and bridegroom Dr Cosmo Lang of York remarked, 'The warm and generous heart of this people takes you today unto itself. Will you not, in response, take that heart, with all its joys and sorrows, unto your own?' His words might have been a prediction of an event which would abruptly change the lives of the Duke and his bride. Lang, as Archbishop of Canterbury, would be an overpowering figure in the Abdication controversy which would culminate in the bleak December of 1936. The Yorks, plunged into kingship, would begin a new partnership between Crown and people.

Some of the principals of those future gloomy weeks were present that day : the handsome Prince of Wales (to be cast in the conspicuous role of petulant King) standing immaculate and alert beside the groom; the Yorks, at that moment believing themselves destined for a royal backwater, unaware then of their eventual dramatic projection into history; and Queen Mary, regal in aquamarine blue stippled with blue crystals. Their actions would determine the fate of a girl yet to be born.

The future Queen Elizabeth II came into this world in the springtime. From the outset she joined together a divided people; they all took the flaxen-haired child to their hearts. Yet few, if any, hailed her as a possible Queen. The Prince of Wales was still only thirty-one, and it was not unreasonable to assume that he would marry. In that case his offspring, whether boys or girls, would stand closer to the throne than his brother's children. Again, the Yorks themselves might have a son who would himself have precedence over sisters in the line of succession.

Thus queenship was remote from the mind when the Christian names of the baby Princess were first mooted. King George v informed Queen Mary, 'I have heard from Bertie about the names, he mentions Elizabeth, Alexandra, Mary. I quite approve and will tell him so, he says nothing about Victoria, I hardly think that necessary.' Perhaps the King was quietly reflecting on the time that Bertie himself was born. The birth – at an outrageous three o'clock in the morning of 14 December 1895 – had sacrilegiously intruded by a few hours into the 'terrible anniversary' of the death of Prince Albert. The Queen's Consort had departed this life thirty-four years previously, yet Victoria still recalled her bereavement with grave and profound solemnity. George v (then the Duke of York) had dutifully telegraphed to his aged grandmother, apologizing for Bertie's violation of such a hallowed day. Ever ready to put pen to paper, the Queen Empress recorded: 'I have a feeling that it might be a blessing for the dear little boy, and may be looked upon as a gift from God'. But George v was never wholly convinced that he had escaped reproach; more than once he ruefully confided that Victoria looked on the birth as 'a personal affront.'

And so the spirit of the indomitable old Empress had at last been 'exorcized'. King George v's first granddaughter duly received the names of Elizabeth Alexandra Mary after her mother, great-grandmother, and grandmother. 'Elizabeth of York sounds so nice too', Bertie had commented when seeking his father's consent. 'And there has been no one of that name in your family for a long time', he added.

True to the simple character of the Yorks the baptism of the infant Princess in the private chapel at Buckingham Palace on 29 May 1926 was an unpretentious ceremony totally stripped of pomp. The beautiful Lily Font, the gold vessel designed in 1840 for Queen Victoria's first child, was brought from

Windsor Castle and filled with water from the River Jordan (the scene of the first known baptism) – a traditional rite dating from the Crusades. Dr Lang, then of York, officiated before six sponsors: the four grandparents, the Princess Royal and the Duke of Connaught, but unfortunately the proceedings were a trifle marred because (so wrote Queen Mary), 'of course poor baby cried'.

The choice of the name Elizabeth for the child to whom destiny would bear the Crown was a coincidence which conjured in the English mind the most romantic of queenly names. But how arrestingly different had been this christening from that of the child's great Tudor namesake. Then, at the Palace of Greenwich, there had been the strident fanfares, the gifts of gold and the dazzling assembly of bishops and mitred abbots. The childhood of the two Elizabeths would contrast too. For the first, offspring of 'the concubine, the Queen', there would be days and nights of fear, even terror: for the second, peaceful happiness would suffuse her scenes of childhood.

King George v himself entered into the role of grandfather with zest. In the child's formative years the elderly monarch would exercise a lasting influence. Of his devotion to his granddaughter there can be no question. It is significant that, on recuperating from his serious lung infection in the winter of 1928–9, King George requested that Lilibet (the way the child pronounced her name) should stay with him at Craigwell, near Bognor. Queen Mary wrote, 'George delighted to see her'. When he resumed writing his journal, it was to 'our sweet little grandchild' that he often referred.

Obviously Glamis, which is said to be the oldest inhabited residence in Britain, formed part of the backcloth to the childhood scene. The most ancient parts of this austere, sandstone fortress, with its secret passages and air of the supernatural, took shape at the turn of the sixteenth century, at the time of Patrick, the first Strathmore Earl. In time Lilibet would learn that the richly colourful story of Glamis ran like a bloodstained thread through much of Scottish history. The brooding fortifications are the perfect setting for the legends of haunted rooms and bygone terror. And when the wraith-like mists creep over the heathery Strathmore valley, the turreted castle has all the spookiness with which it is credited. Commented Sir Walter Scott,

The heavy pile contains much in its appearance, and in the traditions connected with it, impressive to the imagination. It was the scene of a murder of a Scottish king of great antiquity – not indeed the gracious Duncan with whom the name naturally associates itself, but Malcolm II. . . . I was conducted to my apartments in a distant part of the building. I must admit that when I heard door after door shut after my conductor had retired, I began to consider myself as too far from the living, and somewhere too near the dead. . . .

When Lilibet grew older there would be much to explore and stimulate the imagination : for instance, Duncan's Room, King Malcolm's Room and Hangman's Room (where, so the story runs, the last two guests hanged themselves). She would also learn that thick-walled Glamis, loyal to the Stuart cause, had withstood the privations of a Hanoverian siege. The family of those perilous times finally resigned itself to the inevitability of Hanoverian rule. But the relics still survive as memorials to a lost but romantic cause. In the chapel the figure of Christ is seen in the likeness of the sad, dignified Charles I, and memories of the Old and Young Pretenders, both of whom were entertained at Glamis, still linger. The watch which Bonnie Prince Charles left beneath his pillow is testimony to his flight in 1745, and the sword and clothes and the bed in which he slept also recall that dash to freedom.

For the moment Lilibet was too young to realize that the blood of both Stuarts and Hanoverians flowed in her veins; that, in a sense, she symbolized the reconciliation between the two opposing dynasties.

But her ancestry is much more ancient than that; it runs far back in a tortuous line to the misty times of the Anglo-Saxons. In its course there are departures from the male line, which is the normal genealogical approach. Indeed the male line ends with Lilibet's great-great-grandfather, Victoria's Consort Prince Albert of Saxe-Coburg and Gotha. To follow that course is to delve into the history of a minor royal family of Saxony. But by changing to the female line we come to the Hanoverians. Queen Victoria was the granddaughter of George III (who 'gloried in the name of Briton' and as 'Farmer George' endeared himself to the nation with his simple rural tastes). This King, who became blind and mentally unstable, was in turn the great-grandson of George I in whose veins ran some of the blood royal of both England and Scotland.

His accession, however, was due to the Act of Settlement – a parliamentary manoeuvre designed to oust the Catholic Stuarts and their legitimate claims to the throne. George's mother, Sophia, Electress of Hanover, was the daughter of Princess Elizabeth, an offspring of the Stuart James I, but no one could deny that the Old Pretender (the son of James II) and his heir had greater right to the Crown than the Hanoverians. That was why the Strathmores and other ardent Jacobites had bitterly rebelled against political machinations.

The male Hanoverian line becomes involved in the annals of a younger branch of the once powerful Guelph dynasty which left such an indelible imprint on the history of Europe. In the twelfth and thirteenth centuries the mighty Guelphs formed dynastic alliances with England; the turbulent Duke Henry the Lion became the son-in-law of the Plantagenet Henry II (whose desire to gain greater control over the Church led to the murder of Thomas Becket). The Guelph George I and the Whig fraternity, who enthusiastically welcomed his arrival in London, exploited this link with the past, hoping to end the cold apathy of the people and Jacobite hostility.

When she came to study her complex genealogy Lilibet would learn that it was during George's reign that her future status as a constitutional monarch took root in the shrewd mind of Sir Robert Walpole. She would discover, too, that George's mother the Electress Sophia was the daughter of Elizabeth Queen of Bohemia whose father was James I of England and VI of Scotland (the King who wore a padded jacket, fearing an assassin's knife). James, the son of Mary Queen of Scots, was the only Stuart link with Lilibet's ancestry. Through James and his mother Lilibet was descended from both the old Scottish and English royal lines.

Mary Queen of Scots was the daughter of James v, a descendent of Robert, hereditary High Steward of Scotland, who ascended the Scottish throne in 1371 as Robert II by virtue of his mother, Marjorie Bruce, the daughter and heiress of Robert Bruce, hero of Bannockburn. The death of Margaret, the Maid of Norway, while returning to her native Scotland in 1290 had terminated the central line of Scottish sovereigns, thus enabling Robert Bruce, a descendent of a minor offshoot from the twelfth-century David I, to wear the Crown. Further into Scottish history beyond King David drift the shadowy figures of the McAlpine monarchs, among them Shakespeare's Duncan, until the line vanishes in hazy legend.

To pick up the thread of Lilibet's pedigree one must return to James I (who, due to the size of his tongue, slobbered when he spoke, and walked with legs misshapen by rickets). James was the great-grandson of the English Margaret Tudor, the eldest daughter of Henry VII who, by his marriage to Elizabeth of York, ended the brutal Wars of the Roses. Henry's hereditary link with the throne was somewhat frail; he was the senior heir of the Beauforts who were illegitimately descended from John of Gaunt, although they had been legitimatized in 1397. The stronger claim was that of Elizabeth, his wife, the eldest daughter of Edward IV, whose father the Duke of York had triggered off the struggle between Yorkists and Lancastrians. Edward's right to the throne stemmed from his grandmother, Anne Mortimer, the senior representative of Edward III, great-granddaughter and heiress of Edward's son, Lionel Duke of Clarence. Lionel's descendants constituted the senior line of the Angevin kings (later known as Plantagent).

Before the fifteenth-century's confused genealogy, Lilibet's ancestry is less intricate. First came the three Edwards, then Henry III and the profligate John who was forced to seal Magna Carta, the foundation of English liberty. Arriving at the reign of Henry II the male line emanated from the Counts of Anjou, who can be traced to Tortelf the Forester in the ninth century. But on the maternal side, Henry's mother Matilda was the daughter of the scholarly Henry I (nicknamed 'Beauclerc' owing to his erudition) and a granddaughter of the shrewd yet ruthless William the Conqueror. She was also the daughter of Matilda of Scotland, a pious woman who by her union with Henry I restored to vanquished England the old Anglo-Saxon royal line; for she was the great-granddaughter of King Edmund (called Ironside owing to his great physical strength). Edmund, who fought the last battle with the invading Danes, was descended from the heroic scholar Alfred the Great (whose translations from Latin gave the English their first literature).

In this way Lilibet's romantic line goes back through Egbert (generally acknowledged as the first King of the English in 829) to Cerdic, believed to have led the first Saxon invaders to Britain, who died in 534. After that fact ends and fiction begins, for if one accepts the records of Anglo-Saxon chronicles the sovereigns of early times were revered as the sons of gods and were endowed with supernatural powers to fulfil their earthly tasks. Although it is hard to include such deities as Wodin and Thor in Lilibet's ancestral antiquity, at least her forbears can be traced back for almost fifteen hundred years: an illustrious pedigree headed by the sixth-century Cerdic who founded the Saxon dynasty which remained indestructible for more than five centuries. Its chieftains waxed in power, becoming mighty overlords and finally Kings of England.

Perhaps few Londoners knew or even cared that Lilibet was descended from both the old English and Scottish royal lines. To most people she was merely an adorable, fair-haired child as, with her nanny, Mrs Alah Knight, who had been the Duchess of York's own nurse, she rode in an open brougham sent from Buckingham Palace. History pays scant regard to the nurses of our future monarchs. Yet an immense influence is exerted by them in impressionable childhood. When nine years old, Henry VI granted Letters Patent under the Great Seal to his nurse, Dame Alice Butler, 'with licence reasonably to chastise us' should she deem it necessary. In this modern age no royal nanny needs such authorization. Yet the influence she can impose is still tremendous.

In reflective mood the late Duke of Windsor, referring to his own childhood, frankly confessed to the absence of the affection normally bestowed on a child in any good home. Even when servants showed warmth he was never certain if it was genuine or because of his unique status as heir apparent. The affection of his nurse was decidedly questionable. Indeed the after-effects were perhaps traceable into manhood. It seems that this neurotic woman was so obsessed with her young Prince that she could not bear to have him out of her care. Whenever her charge was taken to his parents she would secretly twist his arm so that the tearful Edward was returned to her more promptly. It is most likely that this childhood torture influenced his temperament. After three years the nurse was dismissed, due to her mental instability. But in that time the consequence of her behaviour had had a serious effect on Prince Albert. So badly did she neglect him, feeding him at erratic times, that the gastric complaint from which he suffered in later life perhaps originated in that unhappy period. To his acute dismay it wrecked his career in the Royal Navy when, as Mr Johnson, he saw action against the German High Seas Fleet at Jutland.

Prince Albert ensured that Lilibet would be spared unhappy childhood memories by entrusting her to more sensible care. The daughter of a tenant farmer on the Strathmore estate at St Paul's Waldenbury, the composed Alah brooked no interference, allowing no one to disturb the serenity in playroom or nursery.

The London setting of Lilibet's childhood was 145 Piccadilly – not the most magnificent of the mansions in that affluent quarter. Outwardly there was nothing to indicate the presence of royalty. The lofty grey stone building with balcony and pillared door had been silent and unoccupied for some while before being rented by the Duke, but now life returned. The nursery quarters occupied the upper floor, close to a glass dome where on a circular landing were 'stabled' Lilibet's many toy horses. Her lasting memories would be the red-carpeted floor, the rocking chair reserved solely for Alah, and the glass-fronted toy cupboard (to be used years later by Lilibet's own children). The infant Princess looked out on to the privacy of Hamilton Gardens and, beyond, Hyde Park.

Number 145 housed items which never failed to intrigue the childish mind. In the green-pillared hall were the tusks of the elephant which Papa had shot in Uganda. Fascinating, too, were the bevy of exquisitely dressed dolls, and Jimmie, the Australian parrot who squawked with raucous enthusiasm: 'Jimmie have a drink'. The child gazed in awe at the porcelain Highland figures striding the mantelpiece of the morning room, or waited with blissful anticipation before an astonishing clock, a wedding present to the Yorks from the people of Glasgow. On weekdays, at four three-hourly intervals, a march burst from this amazing timepiece. And, true to the character of the Scottish Sabbath, the clock was stubbornly silent but for the striking of the hour on Sundays. It was an imaginative introduction to the royal pomp and ritual with which she would be identified in later life; for, at the first tinkling notes of the music, George III and his family walked staidly around a dial depicting Whitehall.

The domestic environment in which Lilibet was nurtured in her early years was quiet rather than spectacular. Unlike the sophisticated Prince of Wales the Duke of York shrank from the brittle glitter of life in the twenties, with the result that the smart socialite set regarded the Yorks as a rather dull pair. But even had he desired it, the Duke could not have entertained on any lavish scale, for his allowance would never have permitted it. As it was the modest, home-loving Yorks preferred an unruffled simple existence, sometimes paying an unobtrusive visit to a nearby cinema.

As she grew older Lilibet would ponder on the groups of people who sometimes vanished mysteriously into Papa's library. But the explanation was simple. In those pre-Abdication days Prince Albert used his home as a rendezvous for discussion groups, encouraging representatives of trade unions and managements to try to resolve their problems.

In the first ten years of Lilibet's childhood her father immersed himself in such praiseworthy causes as the Dockland Settlement. He was genuinely distressed by the social chasm which divided rich from poor, and so he financed his own camps which brought together boys from the public schools and the slums.

From the example of her father Lilibet learnt that a major duty of royalty was to involve one's life with that of the people. The process had been initiated by her grandfather who, determined to take his family into the lives of his subjects, encouraged his sons and daughter to serve as his ambassadors. That was how Prince Albert came to take so strong an interest in industrial affairs. The Rev. Robert Hyde, architect of the Industrial Welfare Society, which was designed to foster human relations in industry, rightly pointed out that, although Britain was at the time the world's most industrialized power, visits by royalty to industrial plants were rare. Blunt in manner like his father, Albert, on identifying himself with Hyde's plans, remarked with his usual frankness: 'I'll do it, but I don't want any of that damned red carpet'. These words epitomized his attitude when he wore the Crown and trained his daughter in the subtleties of kingship. One cannot overestimate the influence of the father over the daughter. In consequence rather than being weakened by social and political change – conditions in which the monarchy might easily have withered – the bond between sovereign and people is firmer today than at any time. Elizabeth II is essentially a 'people's Queen'.

♫ 2 An Inglorious Period

When she was four years old Lilibet was joined by a baby sister. For the birth of her second child the Duchess travelled to Glamis in the summer of 1930. A Labour Government was then in power and John Clynes, the Home Secretary, hurried north to confirm the birth. Perhaps the sturdy little Clydesider and erstwhile textile worker was over zealous; his arrival was untimely. In some consternation the Duke wrote to Queen Mary : 'I feel so sorry for Mr Clynes having to be here for so long. I always wanted him to come up when he was sent for, which would have been so much easier.' A disconcerting situation was averted by the initiative of the Dowager Countess of Airlie. To the Duke's relief she invited the Home Secretary to Cortachy Castle, some eight miles distant. There Clynes' patience was taxed for sixteen days, but on the stormy night of 21 August, as lightning inflamed ferine skies, a telephone call summoned him to Glamis. Lashed by the wind, torrential rain streamed down the castle's rugged walls. In such wildness the ghosts of Glamis were said to be most active; among them that of Duncan, and the murdered page with his awesome knocking. Yet nothing disturbed the calm of the Tapestry Room as Princess Margaret Rose was born at 9.22 P.M. – the first royal birth in Scotland since Charles I embarked on a melancholy life at Dunfermline in 1600.

From a turret window Princess Elizabeth saw a vast beacon set ablaze high on the hillside above Glamis to commemorate her sister's arrival. The little newcomer might have thrown Lilibet's autocratic world into ferment; instead Lilibet adopted a protective attitude towards her small sister. After the christening she is credited with the remark: 'I shall call her Bud. You see she is not really a rose yet. She's only a bud.'

Before the Yorks returned to London in October the Duke visited Charles Buchanan, the village postmaster and registrar at Glamis, to register the birth. The Duke signed the name 'Albert' and gave as his address his Piccadilly home.

Back in London Lilibet and her sister lived in an unpretentious and sheltered environment. Happiness was the key-note everywhere. Both the Duke and Duchess made certain of this. In Albert's case he could clearly recall instances that had scarred his boyhood. Childhood had been disrupted as his parents and the court of Edward VII moved about Britain on seasonal migrations. But perhaps the most ineffaceable memories were of his austere father. To his subjects, both in Britain and the Empire, King George V was seen in the guise of a kindly and paternal figure. Basically a keen family man, he was extremely fond of his children. Yet, by general consensus, to his sons and daughters he was often remote and severe. Once, when still the Duke of York, his domineering strictness was commented on by Lord Derby, a mild rebuke which evoked the bluff reply: 'My father was frightened of his mother; I was frightened of my father; and I am damned well going to see to it that my children are frightened of me.' One can surmise that these words were more than tinged with exaggeration. But it is true that this sincerely pious sailor-King (who read his Bible daily) often treated his children as if he still stumped the quarter-deck. The pockets of their sailor suits were sewn to prevent hands from entering them. And woe betide anyone who let stockings slip beneath the knees. To be summarily summoned to his library for a misdemeanour was to become the butt of a livid temper accompanied by the vocabulary of a rough-tongued salt. Being the cynosure of the nation George V held obstinately to the uncompromising standards expected of royalty. He never once wavered and insisted that without fail his children did likewise. Unfortunately, even in his more affable moments, he seemed incapable of transmitting to his children the true measure of his devotion for them.

Nervous and lonely, the shy, serious-minded boy grew up quite unsure of himself. Indeed it is said that he would remain alone in the darkness of a room rather than ask to have the gas lit. Not that – if the anecdote is true – he lacked the family temper; when scolded once for allowing his mind to wander during studies he tugged fiercely at the beard of his German tutor. (In due course, a similar display of anger would be shown during lessons by his daughter Lilibet.)

Maybe it was in the schoolroom that a lifelong misfortune was born. He was naturally left-handed, and King George and Queen Mary, foolishly entertaining the Victorian fallacy that left-handedness was something to be deplored, compelled him to labour against his own inclinations to use his right hand. It is contended that from this time can be traced his distressing nervous stutter. Again, whether it was their desire or not, George v sent David and Bertie to the Naval Training College at Osborne on the Isle of Wight, then to the Royal Naval College at Dartmouth. To the officers also went the brusque dictum: 'Treat them like cadets and make them realize their responsibility.'

Osborne was doubtless a traumatic experience for little Bertie. Never before had he experienced the hurly-burly of so many companions, and it contributed even more to his backwardness. He quickly acquired the derisory name of 'Bat Lugs' (owing to the shape of his ears) and felt the pain of pinpricks from cadets curious to learn if he really possessed blue blood. And in spite of plaintive protests, he was kicked by other cadets who merely wished to brag that they had punched the son of the reigning monarch.

Often starved in early years of parental affection Prince Albert saw to it that there was no such omission in the childhood of Lilibet and her sister. A close personal relationship grew between himself and his daughters. The Duchess of York was equally anxious that the upbringing of Elizabeth and Margaret should be similar to that in any normal affluent family. In her case she drew on the experiences of her own infancy. Apart from two terms spent at a preparatory school in

1 (*Left*) The infant Princess Elizabeth – 'the nation's darling' – riding in an open brougham with her nanny, Mrs Alah Knight. Then third in line to the throne, Elizabeth was destined to become Britain's sixth sovereign queen.

2 Though somewhat severe to his own children, George V ('Grandpa England'), here with Queen Mary, idolised his granddaughter Lilibet. He asked for her companionship at Bognor where he recuperated from his serious illness.

4 (*Below*) Elizabeth and her sister, Margaret, visit the penguins at London Zoo.

5 Princess Elizabeth, then sixteen years old, at a Girl Guide camp at Frogmore, Windsor, in June 1942. She was a member of the Buckingham Palace Company.

7 (*Below*) Glamis Castle, an ancient pile with a bloodstained history, formed one of the childhood settings of Princess Elizabeth.

8 (*Above*) The romance of King Edward VIII and Mrs Wallis Simpson divided the nation. In the crisis bitter condemnation was countered by vehement support from the former unemployed whose lot the King, as Prince of Wales, strove to improve.

INSTRUMENT OF ABDICATION

I, Edward the Eighth, of Great Britain, Ireland, and the British Dominions beyond the Seas, King, Emperor of India, do hereby declare My irrevocable determination to renounce the Throne for Myself and for My descendants, and My desire that effect should be given to this Instrument of Abdication immediately.

In token whereof I have hereunto set My hand this tenth day of December, nineteen hundred and thirty six, in the presence of the witnesses whose signatures are subscribed.

SIGNED AT
FORT BELVEDERE
IN THE PRESENCE
OF

9 (*Right*) The price of a royal liaison. Uncle David's stubborn insistence on marrying the American divorcee led to the Instrument of Abdication in December 1936. Princess Elizabeth of York became Heiress Presumptive.

10 King George VI and Queen Elizabeth with their daughters at Royal Lodge in 1942. The hand which steadied the throne, rocked by the Abdication and its aftermath, was that of Queen Elizabeth, now the Queen Mother.

11 A master monarch with his royal apprentice at Windsor Castle. From the age of ten and a half Princess Elizabeth was groomed with one object – queenship.

12 At her wedding to Prince Philip at Westminster Abbey on 20 November 1947, Princess Elizabeth assumed the name of Mountbatten. However, two months after succeeding to the throne she reverted to the family name of Windsor.

London the Duchess had been taught entirely at home. Moreover her mother Lady Strathmore had supervised the lessons, herself teaching the rudiments of reading and writing. This would be precisely the educational pattern for the two Princesses. The Duchess taught them about God, and the value of prayer, as well as the Bible tales as her mother had related them to her.

To give their children anything like a normal childhood the Yorks had to escape from the prying eyes of public intrusion. At Number 145 inquisitive passengers in the upper decks of passing buses craned their necks, hoping to catch a glimpse of the royal children. And so the Yorks also secured a rural retreat. The decaying Royal Lodge in Windsor Great Park (a grace-and-favour residence) had little to commend it when the Yorks examined it in the autumn of 1931. But Princess Elizabeth would come to accept the Royal Lodge as her true home, even long after her father's accession. Here at Windsor was born her zeal for riding, a passion which had been equally pronounced in certain other queens regnant. Centuries earlier the first Elizabeth had scorned the litter, preferring horseback, and Queen Anne was a keen huntswoman: 'a mighty hunter, like Nimrod', according to Dean Swift. When, after her many pregnancies she grew too fat to ride, she rode to hounds in a light one-seater carriage and, again in the words of Swift, drove 'furiously like Jehu'.

Gardening was another joy to which Elizabeth and her sister were introduced at Royal Lodge. A stone pedestal from a famous Thames landmark, Old Waterloo Bridge, denoted the division between the Princesses' small gardens.

Both at Windsor and Number 145 the nursery quarters of the royal ménage were in the care of four people. Supreme, the kindly Alah ruled firmly over Smith, the nursery maid, Margaret MacDonald, the under-nurse, and her sister Ruby, Princess Margaret's special nurse. In that halcyon world two people would emerge as Lilibet's closest friends right into adult life: her sister and Margaret MacDonald, more commonly known as 'Bobo', an affectionate nickname coined in exciting

23

c

moments when Princess and under-nurse participated in garden games of hide-and-seek, the one leaping out on the other and shouting, 'Boo, boo'.

Miss MacDonald joined the Yorks' domestic staff at the age of twenty; today, a neat, lively Scotswoman in middle age, she has served Lilibet ever since. Ostensibly she is the Queen's dresser, unostentatiously taking care of the royal wardrobe. But that is only one facet of Bobo's role. To the Queen the retiring Miss MacDonald is both an intimate and confidant, tackling many irritations and problems which intrude into a sovereign's life. When the Queen is travelling abroad, Bobo MacDonald is always in her retinue. Indeed the story of Bobo runs like a fairy tale – beginning in a humble home and ending amid the lush magnificence of the foremost residence in the land.

When critics sometimes label the Queen as stuffy, the centre of a clique privileged by accident of birth, they should recall the background of the discreet Margaret MacDonald. Her mother was born in the Sutherland fishing village of Durness, while her father, first a gardener and coachman, rose to nothing higher than a railway surfaceman, living in a little cottage at the crossing at Killearnan.

Another Scotswoman would also have tremendous influence on Lilibet in her formative years. In 1933 the precise and efficient Miss Marion Crawford arrived as resident governess at Royal Lodge. With true cannyness she cautiously accepted a month's trial before finally joining the staff, and then remained in the York household for seventeen years. Dismayed by the squalor of Edinburgh slums the Eton-cropped 'Crawfie', then twenty-one, had conceived the idea of a career in child psychology. But fate planned otherwise.

At Windsor the schoolroom lay on the top floor; at Number 145 in the little boudoir off the drawing room. The Vicomtesse de Bellaigue instructed the royal charges in conversational French, and other tutors taught them German, music, art and dancing. The Duchess of York was unconcerned when Lilibet tussled in vain with mathematics. This placid scene was not always unruffled; there was the occasional incident – as, for instance, when Lilibet explosively revealed the Windsor family's hasty temper while writing French verbs: seizing an inkpot, she impetuously poured the contents over her golden hair.

It was in the schoolroom that the traits which are so marked in Queen Elizabeth today were first noticed. Hard working, conscientious and, no doubt an attribute inherited from her father, intensively painstaking over detail, Lilibet ardently applied herself to try and master whatever task confronted her. Her temperament is shown, as it were, in greater relief when compared with that of her sister. Margaret made no attempt to attend to detail. Light-hearted by nature her approach to studies was more casual; she tended to absorb what her tutors taught her rather than make any strenuous effort to learn. The results of their lessons were just as striking. Although her affection for Lilibet was unquestionable, the mercurial Margaret was clearly determined not to be outdone by her sister. Thus she did the reverse of what Lilibet chose to do. This was expressed in a variety of ways. Both, for instance, studied the piano with Miss Mabel Leander, a pupil of the eminent teacher Leschetizky. Yet whereas Elizabeth had a leaning towards Beethoven and other old masters, Margaret switched to jazz and flamboyant boogie-woogie. Again, when Lilibet approached art with a serious eye, Margaret soared into extravagant fantasy, introducing into her drawings a weird character which she christened 'the Pinkle-Ponkle' – a strange creature which fluttered alarmingly over towns.

Wild pranks were alien to Lilibet's disposition. Yet to pull the plug from the bottom of the boat in which she and a Girl Guide mistress were rowing on the lake at Windsor was typical of Margaret (who, as her father once claimed, 'could persuade the pearl to come out of the oyster'). Even in those days Lilibet revealed the calm, sensible, level-headed qualities which are essential for modern queenship, a fact which was once commented upon by her sister. Scolded by her mother, Margaret quietly observed: 'Isn't it lucky that Lilibet's the elder.'

Lilibet was too young to appreciate the currents that were moving towards social change. Neither could she know that personalities now appearing in the political arena would be prominent in her own reign.

The feverish period after the First World War had ended in a frightening slump. Out of national instability Labour had risen as a third great party. Stanley Baldwin, prescribing protection for Britain's economic ills, had gone to the country. But in the House of Commons the Conservatives were now outnumbered by Labour and Liberal Members and in February 1924, Baldwin had been compelled to resign. As leader of the next biggest party Ramsay MacDonald had formed the first Labour Government, but within a year Baldwin was back at 10 Downing Street. Even so the Labour Party had overtaken the Liberals as a political force. This augured future decline of Liberal fortunes, leaving Conservatism and Labour as the main political contestants.

Winston Churchill, Baldwin's Chancellor of the Exchequer (from whom Lilibet would receive wise counsel in years to come), had raised the external value of the pound – an act which made British goods too costly to buy and merely deepened the depression. Shortly after Lilibet's birth Baldwin had spoken to the nation by the new medium of wireless, a portent of the future, for wireless (and televison) in Lilibet's own reign would be a potent factor in the life of the people and would also help to strengthen the monarchy.

Baldwin had appealed in vain against a General Strike, and in its aftermath the trade unions fared badly; in a Tory-dominated Parliament new legislation sapped the unions' powers and left indelible scars in industrial relations for years to come. Not until the reign of Queen Elizabeth II would the Trade Union Congress grow into a cogent force which no government could ignore.

Meanwhile the Conservatives paid a heavy price for their unsympathetic treatment of the unions. A small majority gain for Labour in 1929 allowed MacDonald to form his second administration, But Labour's period in office coincided with critical and, in a national sense, debilitating times. In September there broke the alarming American slump, and by 1931 Europe was on the brink of financial collapse. Britain was driven off the gold standard, the country sagged under the oppressive social strain of three million unemployed, and in a frantic effort to tackle the crisis MacDonald formed the Coalition or National Government. The young Elizabeth would have been aware that her parents and her uncle the Prince of Wales embarked on tours of the most stricken areas to witness for themselves the social malaise gnawing at the vitals of whole communities.

Thus the childhood of the future Elizabeth II coincided with one of the most inglorious periods in British history. Furthermore, it was the cheerless prelude to the Second World War. While the workless set out on their futile hunger marches, Japan arrogantly invaded Manchuria. In vain an impotent League of Nations protested, and Japan contemptuously resigned from the League, following Germany's example after Hitler's rise to power in 1933.

In Britain itself there was to be a chain of events which would dramatically change the world of the young Elizabeth – and risk toppling the throne. In May 1935 George V and Queen Mary celebrated the Silver Jubilee of their reign. Their appearance in the streets of London sparked off such an outburst of public affection that, after a tour of the East End of London, the King remarked to the Archbishop of Canterbury: 'I had no idea they felt like that about me. I am beginning to think that they must really like me for myself.' Later that month, on Queen Mary's birthday, Lilibet and her sister accompanied their royal grandparents during a drive round north London. Never again would Lilibet ride with Grandpa England. To the British King George had become an institution, but time was running out for him. During June he appeared to revive from a heavy cold, yet by the autumn the bearded face showed signs of acute weariness. The indomitable spirit was failing, and on 10 December the death of his beloved sister Princess Victoria at Coppins, her home near Windsor Forest, struck so deeply that he never seemed to recover. His devotion could be measured by the fact that he had telephoned 'Toria' each morning of his life. Never before had he allowed personal sentiments to eclipse his official duties, yet now he cancelled the State Opening of Parliament which had been planned for that afternoon.

In his Christmas broadcast from Sandringham many people detected in the gruff voice the sick monarch's overwhelming sense of hopelessness. Because their mother was ill with pneumonia Lilibet and Margaret travelled to the sprawling Norfolk mansion without their parents. They knew that Grandpa England was a tired and dejected old man, hunched in his room, wearing his fading Tibetan dressing gown. The King's last Christmas was a dispiriting time. Maybe no one in the house party felt the lowering effect more keenly than Uncle David – worried and irritated no doubt by 'an inner conflict', the consequence of which would drastically reshape Lilibet's destiny.

On 15 January, with the devoted Queen Mary walking by his side, the ailing King rode for a while on his old white pony. But the next day he was confined to his bed. A telephone call to Royal Lodge quickly summoned the Duke of York to Sandringham to assist with the guests. On the 17th the feeble King, making a final significant entry in his diary, wrote succinctly: 'I feel rotten'. Councillors of State were appointed three days later, and on 20 January a distressed Queen Mary recorded: 'At five to twelve my darling husband passed peacefully away – my children were angelic'.

The melancholy news that they would never again see Grandpa England was broken gently to Lilibet and Margaret by their governess. On Tuesday 28 January, from the balcony of Number 145, the Princesses sadly watched the blue jackets haul the gun carriage that bore the draped coffin to Paddington Station for burial at Windsor.

In his final weeks George v, self-styled 'a very ordinary fellow', had reflected gloomily on the future of his dynasty. He was deeply distressed that David, his heir, was not of the same firm mould as the self-effacing, domesticated Albert. The gap between the King and his eldest son had widened appreciably, to the point where conversation was often painfully strained and sometimes almost impossible. The father detested the son's choice of companions and flamboyant night life. For his part David was open in his wholehearted contempt for his father's regularized mode of living, stressing it by acts of rebellion. The King confided in Dr Lang his anxieties about the Prince of Wales. No doubt David's hitherto clandestine romance with the forthright American divorcee Mrs Wallis Simpson was a paramount anxiety.

Meanwhile Queen Mary, who received the news of her son's liaison with frigid disfavour, regarding it as an act of crass stupidity, warned him that there was no alternative but abdication should he stubbornly persist and marry. Her words were echoed by others – among them Stanley Baldwin, the Prime Minister, the Church hierarchy and voices from the Commonwealth. Yet the obdurate Edward VIII, in the words of Lady Hardinge, held tenaciously to his 'secret and private life with a kind of desperation'.

In the royal family the Abdication crisis could not have sounded a more discordant note. It was particularly raucous to the Yorks' ears, for Prince Albert, next in line of succession, viewed with alarm the prospect of being thrust on to the throne. Several times he endeavoured to talk to his brother, but not until 8 December was Albert received at Fort Belvedere. To his horror Edward was inflexible: he would marry. Yet the King was aware of the wave of hostility that would surge through Britain once it was known. Despite his earlier popularity with many subjects, already the malicious attacks in the Press, and the stoning of Mrs Simpson's London home, starkly warned that he would split the nation by remaining on the throne. The King told his brother that he must therefore go into exile. If Baldwin sought someone more akin in temperament and outlook to his father, there was, he said, the Duke of York.

Prince Albert was appalled, stunned by his brother's

renouncement. In the evening he visited his mother to discuss the draft Indictment of Abdication. Finally, engulfed by the awesome future which fate had callously decided for him, the highly strung Duke of York, unable to suppress his emotions, broke down and wept.

On 10 December, King Edward firmly announced his intention to quit the throne. The next night, speaking in a tired voice, he made his final broadcast to the people, declaring, 'A few hours ago I discharged my last duties as King and Emperor, and now that I have been succeeded by my brother, the Duke of York, my first words must be to declare my allegiance to him.'

Earlier the new King had said almost desperately to his cousin, Lord Louis Mountbatten: 'Dickie, this is absolutely terrible. I never wanted this to happen; I am quite unprepared for it. David has been trained for this all his life. I have never even seen a State paper. I am only a naval officer; it is the only thing I know about.' In an effort to raise his spirits, Lord Mountbatten told him: 'George, you are wrong. There is no more fitting preparation for a King than to have been trained in the Navy.' By an odd coincidence King George v, heir to the throne owing to the death of his elder brother the Duke of Clarence had expressed a similar misgiving to Mountbatten's father.

The Duke of York was not legally bound to accept the office of King. Whoever wears the Crown of Great Britain does so under the Act of Settlement. This was passed in 1701 in the reign of William III to safeguard the Protestant succession should both he and his heiress, Princess Anne, die without surviving issue. Because Anne's thirteen children died of congenital syphilis Parliament chose as her successor the Electress Sophia of Hanover, the Protestant granddaughter of James I, thus by-passing the more legitimate claims of Anne's Catholic brother (the Old Pretender) and his son.

When Edward VIII arrived at his irrevocable history-making decision it was necessary for Parliament to amend the Act. But as constitutional lawyers pointed out, no amendment could be made until the politicians had consulted the heir on his personal desires. Although the Duke of York was ready to make the sacrifice inevitably demanded by lifelong kingship he was loathe to commit Princess Elizabeth to the same fate. As yet her tranquil environment and the simplicity of her upbringing were alien to what would be expected of her if she inherited the Crown. It is now generally known that certain people of high authority debated whether or not (by agreement, of course, with the royal family) the Duke of Kent, at that time the only brother of Edward VIII to possess a son, might not be a more suitable candidate. Elizabeth and her father would have been spared a gargantuan task but history now knows that the Yorks to the ultimate benefit of the State – chose not to evade their duties and set their elder daughter firmly on the path to the throne.

As for the Duke, it is doubtful if he ever considered himself. When his brother's abdication loomed darkly, he assured an intimate he would endeavour to restore order from chaos, 'if the whole fabric does not crumble under the shock and strain of it'. Yet he never approached the throne with gusto, as was reflected by the added comment: 'I feel like the proverbial "sheep being led to the slaughter" which is not a comfortable feeling.'

One thing, however, was certain: he had the unstinted support of Londoners. On Abdication night they converged like a human floodtide on Hyde Park Corner and Number 145. In bed with influenza the Duchess rose, curious to learn the cause of the noise. When she realized that the crowd was merely expressing loyalty and affection, she advised her husband to go and speak to the people. Humbly he asked: 'But what am I to say to them?'

To what extent Princess Elizabeth was conscious of the implications for her as a result of Uncle David's abdication is not known. Maybe she knew that the Navy at Portsmouth had taken him away from England on board the *Fury*. Obviously she had some grasp of the situation, for when Margaret asked with innocent curiosity if uncle's head would now be lopped off, she gently admonished her sister, advising her not to talk so foolishly; it merely meant that Papa would henceforth be the King. At the instance of the Queen Miss Crawford had explained to the Princesses that Uncle David wished to marry someone whose divorced husband was still alive. A moral question was involved, and the people had refused to accept her as the Queen.

Princes Elizabeth of York became heiress presumptive shortly after ten o'clock on Thursday 10 December, the time when Edward VIII quit the throne by signing the fifteen documents of the Instrument of Abdication. As he wrote the final signature the studious Elizabeth was most probably changing from a history to a poetry lesson. She too was figuring in the shape of history. But to what degree she was conscious of it perhaps she will never reveal. Yet after recording her swimming lesson she wrote 'Abdication Day' in capital letters on a sheet of Buckingham Palace writing paper.

The prospect of never again being known as Princess Margaret of York did not appeal to Elizabeth's six-year-old sister. 'I was Margaret of York and now I am just Margaret', she pouted. Moreover, she had learnt how to spell 'York'. It is recorded that Princess Elizabeth 'said less because she knew more'. But she was not happy at the thought of living in Buckingham Palace, asking that a tunnel should be built from the Palace to Number 145 so that she could return each evening.

♦ 3 Royal Apprentice

On Saturday afternoon 12 December 1936 at Marlborough House, the home of her grandmother Queen Mary, Princess Elizabeth witnessed her father's proclamation at nearby St James's Palace. There she watched the ancient pageantry in Friary Court that transformed her father into 'our own Lawful and Rightful Liege Lord, George the Sixth'. In that historic moment she too had been elevated, to his heir presumptive.

If she did not know it then, one day she would realize that the legality of her own rank also arose from the Electress Sophia of Hanover. The early eighteenth-century Parliament had decreed that Sophia should be succeeded by her 'heirs general' for all time, assuming, of course, that they were Protestants. Whereas Elizabeth was heiress at the age of ten, Sophia was seventy-two years old when Parliament chose her to succeed Queen Anne. Determined to wear the British Crown she lived by sheer willpower to be eighty-four but rather cruelly death deprived her of her inheritance by a couple of months.

Today Sophia is virtually forgotten, yet Princess Elizabeth – like every monarch who has occupied the British throne since 1714 – has done so as the heir general of this German princess who has now faded into the haziness of time. In the normal sense, an heir general means the eldest son of the oldest male line. Yet if the sovereign has no son, or descendant of a son, to succeed him, his daughters and their issue take precedence over his own brothers.

Under English law, however, there is no primogeniture among sisters. Should there be intestacy a father's estate is shared equally and a peerage goes into abeyance. This ruling applies just as much to the daughters of a King, but in practice neither the Crown nor kingdoms can be apportioned.

At one point constitutionalists probing the legal niceties queried the position of Elizabeth and Margaret under the Act of Settlement. Should not the sisters jointly share the throne? Quite rightly intellectual speculation was swiftly squashed and good sense prevailed. Sir John Simon, the Home Secretary, told the House of Commons that: 'In the event of her father's death, Princess Elizabeth will succeed to the throne as sole heir'. This of course presumed that the Queen would not bear a son. If that happened Elizabeth would be replaced by her brother because he would be the heir *apparent*, the visible heir, for nothing but death could deprive him of his entitlement to the Crown. In the meantime, therefore, Princess Elizabeth remained the heir *presumptive*: she would inherit the Crown *presuming* that no heir apparent was born. This was not legal hocus-pocus, as history had already testified. Princess Mary, for instance, was heir presumptive to Henry VIII for twenty-one years. Then, to his joy, the King's consort was delivered of a son and heir apparent: the future Edward VI. Only on the latter's death did the Princess become Mary I.

Whatever the future held, from the age of ten and a half Princess Elizabeth was groomed specifically for queenship. To some extent her first lesson was to be taught the significance of the coronation ritual. When Hitler and Mussolini threatened to convulse Europe George VI agreed to be crowned on the date fixed for his brother, 12 May 1937. To help Elizabeth to understand the coronation Queen Mary delved into her many possessions, producing a concertina-style model some thirty feet long, of the procession at George IV's coronation. Soon Elizabeth familiarized herself with the aspects which enrich the coronation scene, a knowledge which was enhanced by appropriate reading in the schoolroom.

But nothing could equal her father's gift. One evening in his study the King presented her with a 'special book' bound in beige linen, bearing her title and name embossed in gold. It was her private copy of the illustrated 'Order of the Service of the Coronation'. From this she mastered the complexities of what is perhaps the world's most intricate religious ceremony. Elizabeth took the matter seriously but Margaret regarded it as an occasion for fun. At tea-time at Buckingham Palace, donning coronet and purple robe, she would strut with lofty air, walking stick in hand, claiming that she was 'Johnnie Walker'.

Characteristically Elizabeth thought fit to record her parents' coronation. Still preserved in the Royal Library at Windsor is her personal account written in red pencil in a ruled government-issue notebook: 'To Mummy and Papa. In Memory of Their Coronation. From Lilibet.' An extract reads: 'At five o'clock in the morning I was woken up by the band of the Royal Marines striking up just outside my window. I leapt out of bed and so did Bobo. We put on dressing-gowns and shoes and Bobo made me put on an eiderdown as it was so cold and we crouched in the window looking on to a cold misty morning. There were already some people in the stands and all the time people were coming to them in a stream with occasional pauses in between. Every now and then we were hopping out of bed looking at the bands and the soldiers. At six o'clock Bobo got up and instead of getting up at my usual time I jumped out of bed at half-past seven. . . .'

Later, in Westminster Abbey, in the royal gallery over the tomb of Anne of Cleves, Elizabeth watched the crowning of her father, not knowing that fifteen years hence she too would be the cynosure of the thousand-year-old ritual.

The coronation excitement subsided and the Princess returned to the more placid air of the schoolroom. Elizabeth's studies were now conforming to a specific pattern in which the King himself participated. Having committed his daughter to the inescapable task of queenship, he made every conceivable effort to equip her to cope with it. Whenever possible, in his study each evening he discussed his activities of that day, enlightening her on particular aspects of his duties and their place in the affairs of state.

It has been said that, owing to the relatively early death of King George VI, Princess Elizabeth was ill prepared to succeed him. The contrary is the case. Perhaps never in the history of the British monarchy has an heir been trained so intensively and meticulously. For fifteen years she was the royal apprentice to a master King. In that time a sane relationship between father and daughter made that between some sovereigns and their heirs look like grotesque caricatures. It had been traditional for factions to exist in Hanoverian reigns. The rivalry was worsened by entanglements in the bitterness of political strife. The King would favour one group and the house of the Prince of Wales tended to be the hotbed of intrigue of its opponents. Fortunately the Court today cannot dabble in politics.

But even Queen Victoria foolishly denied her heir apparent real access to matters of state, largely because her consort Prince Albert scorned the intellectual capacity of his son. Although Victoria had intended that the future Edward VII should be trained early for his kingly role, her immoderate devotion to the Prince Consort warped her outlook towards her child. The Queen had an almost fanatical desire to see him resemble his angelic father 'in every respect, both in body and mind'. Regrettably, in the Queen's view, the son never could measure up to the mental stature of her husband.

On Prince Albert's death it was expected that his erstwhile functions would be undertaken by the son. It was even rumoured that the Queen Empress would abdicate in favour of the Prince of Wales. Such reports were baseless, and Edward would be in his sixtieth year by the time of his accession. To Victoria, Edward was totally incapable of fulfilling the duties exercised by his father. Her withdrawal from public gaze to become the 'Widow of Windsor' left Edward even more remote from state affairs. For almost forty years after Prince Albert's death Edward was even debarred from organized duties. Against these frustrations one must set Queen Victoria's complaints about her son's indiscretions. On the other hand it could be argued that Edward's shortcomings sprang from 'a position which never allowed him responsibility or forced him into action'.

Similarly the relationship between George v and his heir was anything but ideal. At first the Prince of Wales represented the King on travels abroad but as the son matured, the tendency to impose responsibilities diminished. The Prince of Wales was thirty-one when in 1925 he returned from his final official tour. From then onwards his status barely exceeded that of his sister and brothers. He was not forbidden to enter into discussions with the Ministers, but he was conscious that it would be an unpopular move. Years later came the plaintive disclosure : 'At the same time, in a manner I have defined, I was expected to remain conversant with all that was going on in the world and to give the impression of being knowledgeable and well-informed.' As in the case of the earlier Edward he did not escape his father's strictures. Some of these were justified, due primarily to his style of living, yet it can be asked if this was not the offspring of frustration.

One mentions these instances to define the relationship between George VI and his daughter. As a royal apprentice, Princess Elizabeth could never complain of the lack of opportunity to assume her role in the nation's affairs. Both George VI and his father had many traits in common but differed glaringly in one respect. George V allowed his life to be hidebound by tradition and convention to the point where he found change intolerable. His son differed in that although he did not necessarily approve of change he philosophically accepted its inevitability and adapted his life accordingly. This was a lesson passed on to his daughter. Moreover, apart from instructing her in the subtleties of kingship, he instilled his credo that it is 'one of my main jobs in life to help others when I can be useful to them.'

In those late 1930s there would be a stridency in the life of Princess Elizabeth, as in the lives of millions of others. In the early summer of 1937 Hitler and Mussolini created their vaunted Rome-Berlin axis. The hysterical ranting of the dictators grew more threatening. The Jackboots were on the march. There was the rape of Czechoslovakia and when Nazi bombs screamed down on Warsaw in 1939 Britain was at war.

The royal family were at Balmoral on that fateful September day. For a while Elizabeth and Margaret remained at Birkhall on the Scottish estate, but early in 1940 they travelled to Royal Lodge. On 12 May, when the Nazis directed their fury on Belgium, the Queen telephoned from Buckingham Palace ordering the Princesses to go to the greater security of Windsor Castle. When there was danger of an invasion of London itself the Cabinet formulated a complex plan to whisk the King and his family to the west country. Picked officers and men of the Guards and the Household Cavalry were assigned to hurry the party along a predetermined route in cars marked with secret code signs. But the Nazis never landed, although their bombs fell on the capital, some dropping on the Palace itself. Once, while in a sitting room above the broad quadrangle, the King and Queen saw the bombs falling and were unable to take refuge.

Princess Elizabeth and her sister stayed at Windsor for the rest of the war, living in the thick-walled Lancaster Tower with its winding staircase built in the reign of Henry VII. At night they were joined by their parents who secretly left London in an armoured car. Disliking its claustrophobic interior, the Queen often contrived to clutter up the car with personal items, thus leaving no space for herself so that she could travel in one of the royal Daimlers. Sometimes at weekends, attending to official documents in his red dispatch boxes, the King resumed his practice of training Elizabeth in what was required of monarchy.

By now she had received detailed lessons on the constitution. To the King's notice had come the name of Clarence Henry Marten. This mild-mannered, rather Pickwickian personality (who was later knighted), had achieved distinction in the scholastic world as historian and writer of history textbooks. As he was Vice Provost of Eton College just across the Thames from Windsor Castle, it was convenient for him to give

Elizabeth guidance in all matters concerning constitutional history. For the young Princess Mr Marten was the ideal instructor. She had long shown a literary bent and in his book *On the Teaching of History* her affable tutor had written that history 'provides an admirable background for English composition ... a vehicle for the training of the memory, the cultivation of the imagination, the development of balanced judgement...'.

It is highly likely that his individual system of teaching and the knowledge which he imparted had a beneficial influence on his young student in later life. A key to his success is found in *The Groundwork of British History* (written jointly with George Townsend Warner) in which he described his attempts to develop in a child's mind 'the faculties of understanding and reason rather than mere memory; and to make boys think why this happened and what the consequences were'.

Constitutional history is the hard core of history, showing over a long period of time the development of the institutions which fix the design of society. Such are Parliament, the Church, the Monarchy, the Law Courts, civic organization and everything which has a direct bearing on the mass of the people. In Britain the roots of the institutions go deep – extending to the thirteenth century and in cases even earlier.

Princess Elizabeth's ancestry goes back at least eleven centuries. Throughout that time – with a gap of only eleven years (from 1649 to 1660, after Oliver Cromwell ousted Charles I) – there has been an unbroken line of Kings and Queens. The monarchy is Britain's second oldest institution – far older than Parliament (some seven hundred years), and of remoter origin than its Courts of Law (eight hundred years); and both are offshoots of the monarchy. Only the See of Canterbury is of greater antiquity (some thirteen hundred years). The only other institution in Europe which is older than the British monarchy is the Papacy.

From this it is apparent that the young Princess, to comprehend the purpose and significance of queenship, had to familiarize herself with the complexities of the constitution.

39

D

No other country is so richly endowed in constitutional history as Britain and the one-time British Empire. Under the expert tuition of Mr Marten she learnt how her future high office was intricately woven into the life of the nation; moreover, that monarchy was meaningless unless it was seen in its relationship with the Ministers of State, Members of Parliament, the judges and sheriffs, officers of the services – indeed, down to the humblest of the electorate who, because of their right to vote, figure in the constitution. Although Princess Elizabeth was baffled by mathematics, she grappled efficiently with such complicated subjects as the evolution of a self-governing dominion, India and the India problem, the national expenditure before 1939 and during the war, and colonial matters. Together with constitutional history Mr Marten encouraged discussion on current affairs, arising usually from press articles or chance observation. For instance, the ploughing of an area of Windsor Great Park as part of the national food production inspired the Princess to study the growth of English agriculture. When necessary she illustrated her exercise books with maps or diagrams.

War had made it imperative for the Princess to intensify her training for queenship. With all the current dangers there was the possibility that the King himself could be a casualty (Buckingham Palace was bombed nine times). Consequently it was the lot of the senior royal prince who was not overseas – invariably the Duke of Gloucester – to be constantly ready to fill the role of Regent on behalf of his niece should the King die or become incapable of discharging his duties.

But after 21 April 1944 this emergency plan was unnecessary; Parliament amended the Regency Act, enabling the Princess to be a Councillor of State when eighteen. The royal apprentice was now not only King George's heir, but also in certain eventualities his understudy. As in the case of George III (a victim of porphyria) and his heir the future George IV, should serious illness befall the King the Princess would now by statute assume virtually all the sovereign's powers. But should he be absent from Britain a Council of State would exercise the royal prerogative in his stead.

In addition to the Princess the Council was composed of the Queen, the Duke of Gloucester, the Princess Royal and Lady Southesk (granddaughter of Edward VII): that is, the Queen and the four adults of the royal family closest to the throne. If the Queen accompanied the King then Princess Elizabeth would automatically be head of the Council. For security reasons it could never be reavealed at the time, yet on several occasions the Princess served as a Councillor while her father visited his troops abroad.

In July 1944 the King bestowed on the Princess armorial bearings, a sign that his elder daughter was truly a public personality in her own right. Many thought that the King would create her Princess of Wales, a decision which rested solely on the sovereign. But such hopes, particularly of the patriotic Welsh, were not fulfilled. However, there was good reason and precedent for this. From the reign of Edward III the title has been the birthright of no one but the heir apparent, usually the sovereign's eldest or only son.

On two occasions a sovereign's grandchildren – the future Richard II and George III – received this dignity when they became heir apparent after their fathers' death. Yet never has it been conferred on any heir presumptive (either male or female). Mary, the daughter of Henry VIII, was referred to as Princess of Wales, but this could have been nothing more than a courtesy title. On her father's instructions she presided over her Court at Ludlow and was the nominal head of the Principality's Government. Yet there were no Letters Patent. Furthermore, there was no problem in later conferring the title upon her brother Edward, then unborn.

If George VI had strayed from centuries of custom, doubtless the title would in due course have lost its original significance. An heir presumptive would claim the dignity, wrongly depriving the King's son yet to be born. When people agitated to have Princess Elizabeth created the Princess of Wales, King George publicly announced that he did not anticipate any alteration in her title. Anyway, as he told the Queen, it would be folly to bestow the title normally identified with the wife of the Prince of Wales, adding: 'Her own name is so nice.'

Other distinctions accorded to the heir apparent on which there can be no argument are his ennoblement to the Dukedom of Cornwall and the Earldom of Chester. The Dukedom was first conferred on the Black Prince in 1339 and under its charter the Duchy can be possessed by no one save the monarch's eldest son. As such he ranks as head of the Second Estate of the realm, the temporal peers in the House of Lords. If an heir presumptive was designated Countess of Chester, and an heir apparent subsequently came into being, the peerage might easily drift away from the royal family through marriage and subsequent inheritance. Custom over the centuries can be as binding as an Act of Parliament and has decreed that no one but the monarch's son or grandson can become Earl of Chester.

Not until her marriage to Prince Philip Duke of Edinburgh was Princess Elizabeth ennobled. To that extent there was a parallel with Queen Anne; marrying her before her accession her husband the dull-witted Prince George of Denmark received the English ennoblement of the Dukedom of Cumberland.

The romance between Princess Elizabeth and Prince Philip, then a handsome, flaxen-haired lieutenant in the Royal Navy, flourished at Windsor Castle in the grim years of the war. But at first it met with little enthusiasm from the King. Not that Philip was not eminently suitable on grounds of birth. He was a grandson of Prince William of Denmark who, in 1863 through British, French and Russian pressure, had founded a new dynasty as King George 1 of Greece. Philip had been born on 10 June 1921 on the island of Corfu, the son of Prince Andrew, who was the fourth son of George 1 and the youngest brother of the reigning King Constantine.

Through the maternal line he was the great-great-grandson of Queen Victoria and therefore the third cousin of his future wife. The Grand Duke Louis of Hesse and Princess Alice, the Queen Empress's second daughter, were his great-grandparents.

A daughter of this union, Princess Victoria of Hesse, married Prince Louis of Battenburg, her cousin, who, securing British citizenship, rose to be Admiral of the Fleet and the First Sea Lord. Then came the First World War and public hostility to this one-time German princeling. He therefore anglicized his name to Mountbatten and George v created him the Marquess of Milford Haven. In due course Alice, his eldest daughter, became Princess Andrew of Greece, and Philip's mother.

Despite drama and sadness from the outset it seemed that fate had decreed that Philip would one day be the consort of a Queen. Not long after he was born the Greeks rashly waged war on Turkey and suffered the destruction of their army. Revolutionaries tumbled Constantine from his throne and in a terrible bloodbath Prince Andrew, a corps commander, escaped solely through the mediation of the British and the Vatican. But he was banished for life. Borne away on a British cruiser Prince Andrew and his family joined the colony of aristocratic emigrés in Paris. But gradually the family's resources dwindled. Princess Andrew was reduced to running an arts and crafts shop in the French capital, and Philip was despatched to England to the care of Lady Milford Haven and his uncle, Lord Louis Mountbatten.

Princess Elizabeth of York and Prince Phillip of Greece had known each other from childhood, often meeting at Brooke House, the Mountbattens' London penthouse home in Park Lane. Some years elapsed and both were adolescents when the friendship was renewed. Sailing in the royal yacht George VI took his family to Dartmouth in July 1939, but an epidemic of measles and chicken-pox prevented the Princesses from attending some of the functions. To while away the time they played croquet in the captain's garden with certain cadets, among whom was Cadet Captain Prince Philip. Of that reunion it has been said that Elziabeth thought Philip rather too self-assertive. For his part Philip, five years older than Elizabeth, regarded her as somewhat immature.

Their sentiments changed in the precarious years of the war, while Philip was on leave in London. As the news gradually leaked to the press there was widespread comment, for although Philip had been reared in the British mould, to many Britons he was still an alien. Rightly or wrongly it was felt that he could never be tolerated as a future consort. The King of the Hellenes enthused over the prospect of an engagement between Elizabeth and Philip, but George VI had at first not been enthusiastic. He did not object to Philip; indeed in the King's view Philip had a dynamic personality and thought 'about things in the right way', but his daughter, he reasoned, had met too few eligible young men and should not at that stage be committed.

When the King grew less adamant he pointed out that if Philip was ever to wed the heiress to the throne he must first win the plaudits of the people and present himself to the public as an Englishman. Naturalization, which meant total renunciation of his claim to the Greek throne, was imperative. At the same time it would yield an additional asset, for it would make him eligible to seek a permanent commission in the Royal Navy which his present status prohibited.

At the end of 1944 the King of the Hellenes gave his blessing to this proposal. All that now remained were the formal discussions with a pliant Home Office. But the irritations of diplomatic complications intervened. Greece had been rent by civil war. Churchill and Eden had visited Athens on Christmas Day 1944, extracting from the turmoil a fragile peace and the appointment of Archbishop Damaskinos as Regent. But was the King of the Hellenes ever to be allowed to return to his throne? In London officialdom was hesitant; to grant naturalization to a member of the Greek royal family might incur a fierce political backlash if it seemed that Britain wholeheartedly shored up the royal cause. On the other hand it might also be thought that the future of the royal family seemed so gloomily precarious as to need sanctuary in Britain.

In 1946 the King of the Hellenes went back to Greece, but naturalization for Philip was again refused for fear that it might be an awkward embarrassment so soon after the restoration. Eventually, at the end of the year Philip was finally permitted to seek naturalization. But what name should he now assume? George VI suggested that he should be known as 'His Royal Highness Prince Philip', but to the King's unconcealed pleasure he preferred to forego a princely title in favour of a naval rank. Because the royal families of Denmark and Greece bear no family name, at the instance of the Home Secretary Mr Chuter Ede, Philip took his mother's name; hence Lieutenant Philip Mountbatten RN.

King George VI and his family were touring South Africa at the time naturalization was at last finalized. The King, however, was in no haste to sanction the bethrothal until he returned to Britain. His anxiety that the Princess might have been too hasty in her decision was still not eradicated. However, on 10 July 1947, to the delight of the people, the King announced his consent.

Time would ratify his wise decision. Both in her capacity as heiress presumptive and later as Queen, Elizabeth would be strongly sustained by her husband. The talents which Prince Philip was to offer to the service of Britain and the Commonwealth were a lively appreciation of a problem (the gap, for instance, between education and industry, or the lack of adventure for modern youth in an industrialized life), good sense and a practical attitude to a solution. His precise, humorous way of expressing his thoughts aloud – with the result that he injects vitality into, say, science or industry – was to win widespread appeal.

A typical comment was his reply to a point raised at a foreign press association luncheon in London. The questioner asked about the monarchy and its true place in relation to the problems of Britain today. 'What you are implying', Philip said, 'is that we are rather old-fashioned. Well, it may easily be true. I do not know. One of the things about the monarchy and its place, and one of its greatest weaknesses in a sense, is that it has to be all things to all people and, of course, it cannot do this when it comes to being all things to all people who are traditionalists and all things to all people who are iconoclasts. We therefore find ourselves in a position of compromise, and we might be kicked on both sides. The only thing is that if you are very cunning you get as far away from the extremists as you possibly can because they kick harder. I entirely agree that we are old-fashioned: it is an old-fashioned institution. The interesting thing about monarchy is that it is not a monopoly of old people.'

When the King announced the betrothal Philip's mother, Princess Alice of Greece, supplied the engagement ring, highly prized because it had been a gift to her by her late husband. The news of the match was received enthusiastically by the people, and the wedding in Westminster Abbey on 20 November 1947, for which the Princess wore a bridal gown studded with ten thousand pearls, cast a sparkle on the drab, blitzed London scene. On the eve of the marriage, the King created Philip a Knight of the Garter, Baron Greenwich, Earl of Merioneth and Duke of Edinburgh, and gave him the title of His Royal Highness.

With the Duke, Princess Elizabeth, representing the British people, embarked on the first of many informal visits overseas (in time she would be the most travelled monarch in all history). In Paris she opened a display of *Eight Centuries of British Life*. One exhibit in particular which amused her was the top hat of her great-grandfather displayed beneath glass. Then they travelled to Greece, and in the autumn of 1957 journeyed to Canada and the United States. It was on this tour that Philip conspicuously displayed an innate talent for popularizing the monarchy. Elizabeth won the cordiality of the crowds with her graciousness and friendly charm, but it was her husband who adroitly cast his spell over the masses.

In the main Elizabeth had led a protected, sheltered life, away from even the fringe of ordinary people. For Philip it was totally different. War had rudely deprived him of the rarefied air of Court life. Although he could not be placed in the category of the mass of the people at least he was much nearer to them, understanding their language more thoroughly. Perhaps more important he was more sensitively attuned to the subtleties of public reason. Thus he sensed the moods and demands of the crowds. Meeting them with an arresting personality and spontaneous wit. He was always the reassuring figure behind the Princess, investing her with confidence, smoothing out whatever problem arose. The Duke had assumed his exacting role as consort with a bold self-reliance: so much so that an American reporter generously observed that 'Philip could run for Congress on the Republican ticket in Texas and win'.

The King's deteriorating health inevitably added to the duties imposed on his understudy Elizabeth. Long hours at work – indeed, maybe he was overzealous in his task – and the anxieties of a harassed reign were exacting their toll. In the latter part of 1948 George VI was stricken by an arterial ailment of the legs (which almost resulted in amputation). But he recovered sufficiently to witness the christening of Prince Charles, his first grandchild, on 15 December at Buckingham Palace.

However, illness stalked him relentlessly and by the following March it was manifest that an operation for lumber sympathectomy was unavoidable. The doctors tried to persuade him to have the operation at the Royal Masonic Hospital, but he replied that he had never 'heard of a King going to a hospital before', and so a room at the Palace was adapted as a surgical theatre.

Early in 1951 he was well enough to participate in the service at St Paul's Cathedral to mark the opening of the Festival of Britain. As humorous as ever he confided to the smattering of people around him that the Festival 'Skylon' was like the nation's economy: 'it had no visible means of support'. Yet he was too sick to set out on a prearranged tour of Australasia. Once again Princess Elizabeth had to stand in as his deputy.

Thus on 31 January 1952 the tired, ailing monarch stood bare-headed, waving to Elizabeth and Philip as they set off for Kenya, Ceylon, Australia and New Zealand. His face was worn and sad, as if he sensed that he would never see his elder daughter again. From Heathrow he was driven to Sandringham for what was intended to be a rare and much needed rest. On 5 February pleasant weather drew him out of doors with his dogs for his favourite pastime, shooting. After dinner that night he amused himself with a jigsaw puzzle and Princess Margaret played to him on the piano before he left for his room about 10.30. The King was reading a magazine when footman Daniel Long took him a cup of cocoa at eleven o'clock.

At 7.30 the next morning the King lay as if in a tranquil sleep from which James Macdonald, his assistant valet, could not wake him. Coronary thrombosis had ended his life, maybe not long after midnight. Hurriedly summoned, the Queen kissed the forehead of her lifeless husband and despite her grief was heard to say: 'We must tell Elizabeth. We must tell the Queen.'

Unconscious of her father's death Elizabeth had been Queen for several hours, for under the constitution the throne can never be left vacant. She had spent the night some 4,500 miles away, near the Equator in a hut called Treetops in an enormous figtree, watching wild animals drink at a jungle pool. On her return to Sagan Lodge, Nyeri, a wedding gift from the people of Kenya, at almost three o'clock Kenya time that afternoon Prince Philip told her the tragic news. Without warning she was no longer Princess.

When she stood again on British soil on the afternoon of 7 February, seven days after she had waved farewell to her father, she did so as Elizabeth the Second. The next morning she walked along the snow-strewn path from her home, Clarence House, to nearby historic St James's Palace, there signing her oath of accession. In the afternoon she left for Sandringham and for a while knelt alone beside the body of her father, now lying in his coffin of Sandringham oak. The Norfolk squire was at rest; so too was the King who had initially sat on a shaky throne yet had left it secure for his daughter. When he had accepted the Crown which his brother had thrust aside, Princess Helen Victoria, an ageing cousin, had asked rather anxiously if he felt competent to cope with kingship. 'I do not know', he had replied with typical candour, 'but I am going to do my best.' His brother's defection had been a crisis for the monarchy unparalleled in modern times. It was the opinion of Sir Arnold Wilson, MP, that if the House of Commons had voted on the issue, some forty or fifty Members would have favoured a Republic. Thus Princess Elizabeth might never have reached the throne.

The crash of the monarchy was averted partly because Clement Attlee, leader of the Socialist opposition, creditably refused to make political capital and because Edward VIII honourably declined to create a King's Party. Yet perhaps of more far-reaching importance were the then hidden qualities of his successor. Ostensibly, at the outset George VI impressed as a rather pathetic recruit for kingship and many of his subjects must have feared for the worst. Yet amazingly 'George the Good' restored firmness and stability to the throne despite the devastating years of the Second World War, an unstable climate in which, as history has often illustrated, the foundations of monarchy tend to rot.

Perhaps this thought persisted relentlessly in the mind of the Duke of Windsor as he walked behind his brother's bier on the day of burial. At least, he would write later:

The constant strain to which George VI was subjected . . . was augmented towards the end of his reign by the pain and anguish of failing health and two major operations. And I am not insensible of the fact that through a decision of mine he was projected into sovereign responsibilities that may at first have weighed heavily upon him – it fell to him to carry the monarchy successfully through the most difficult phase of the social revolution which began in my grandfather's time . . . he lived long enough to see that totalitarianism in any form is not congenial to the British national character. But what must have been equally satisfying to him was to see his eldest child grow into womanly maturity; to see her married to a young man of resolute character and endowed with a modern mind, and to see the succession firmly assured. . . .'

On 15 February the body of King George VI was buried in the

vaults of the Renaissance St George's Chapel, Windsor, where already lay the remains of nine ancestors. In keeping with the character of the dead monarch there was no ostentation in this ancient, bannered shrine of Cotswold stone. Apart from the simple acts peculiar to a monarch's death, the burial rite was the same as that of many of his subjects. By tradition the Lord Chamberlain 'broke' his white staff, placing one piece on the coffin – a gesture signifying that his authority had ended with the sovereign's death. Then the Queen laid a red silk square, the King's Colours of the Grenadier Guards (of which King George VI had been Colonel-in-Chief) across the head of the coffin. Finally the Archbishop of Canterbury intoned the committal, and as the body of her father vanished slowly through the cavity in the choir floor, Elizabeth II sprinkled it with Windsor soil from a silver bowl. Her gesture marked the ending of a notable reign and the dawn of the second Elizabethan Age.

ॐ 4 Crown and Regalia

The accession of Queen Elizabeth II was unique in English history. Before her no daughter had immediately succeeded her father; moreover, never before had a reigning monarch specifically groomed his daughter as his understudy and natural successor. Queen Victoria, who had opined that women were ill-suited to the onerous duties of monarch ('... we women, if we are to be good women, feminine and amiable and domestic, are not fitted to reign ...'), was the niece of George IV and William IV, who preceded her. With that exception all other Queens of England were the daughters of kings. Yet the half-sisters, the Tudors Mary I and Elizabeth I wore the Crown after their younger brother Edward VI, and not after their father Henry VIII.

If the Whigs had not tampered with hereditary right, the Stuart Mary II, the wife of William of Orange, would never have occupied the throne after her father, the Catholic James II. In the Glorious Revolution of 1688, when the deposed James fled the country (dropping the Great Seal in the Thames in his haste), he was replaced by William and Mary (who were later succeeded by Mary's sister, Anne). At no time was Mary II her father's legitimate heiress. That right was vested in his son whom the Jacobites fiercely hailed as James III of England and VIII of Scotland, and who was dubbed the Old Pretender by the Whigs. Therefore neither Mary nor Anne wore the Crown by hereditary right but solely by the machinations of Parliament.

The Empress Maude, the daughter of Henry I, was never crowned, and has never been accepted as a queen regnant. True, with the dramatic loss of his son in the wrecked White

Ship in 1127, Henry had presented Maude (or Matilda) as England's next sovereign, but she devoted her energies to the struggle with King Stephen. Her niche in history is as the mother of the renowned Henry II.

Born in 1796 Charlotte, the daughter of the future George IV and his consort Caroline of Brunswick, was expected by the British to be their eventual Queen. This was inevitable for, owing to the implacable breach of her parents, the birth of a son was out of the question. But she became the spouse of Prince Leopold of Saxe-Coburg (who was destined to be the first King of the Belgians), and tragically succumbed at the age of twenty-one in giving birth to a stillborn child.

This unfortunate Princess is the nearest comparison with the young Elizabeth II. But the similarity is limited. As Prince Regent Charlotte's licentious father commendably safeguarded his daughter from the laxity and corruption of his Court, yet it is doubtful if he ever taught her the necessities of queenship. As for the earlier George, unlike King George VI, he was loathed by the people for his debauchery and prodigality. The keen anticipation with which ordinary folk awaited Charlotte's accession was born largely of the hope that it would herald happier times. It was a time of shocking rising costs and poverty, yet despite the misery of thousands – caused chiefly by the Napoleonic Wars – the King freely squandered the nation's money and obstructed reform. In contrast George VI justly merited his people's affection. Today it is bestowed on his daughter.

In Britain, this bond between the modern sovereign and people is the real foundation for the monarchy's popularity and continuance. Yet the bond is indefinable. Doubtless a good deal of its strength is drawn from history; for even though the present-day institution of monarchy differs substantially from that of centuries ago, the ritual and pomp have continued over the years. It links the immediate present with an eventful past. It is living proof that over the long period of time the nation has continued in good times and bad and therefore provides reassurance for the future.

Perhaps no ritual strikes a more stirring note of confidence than the coronation ceremony at the outset of a reign. The reason is that it is rich in symbolical appeal and meaning. However, the involvement of the Commonwealth of Nations (and the many complexities that this involves) has to some extent robbed the ceremonial of some of its earlier significance. Nowadays some twelve months elapse between the accession and the coronation to allow the various countries concerned to complete arrangements. Yet originally the coronation was observed immediately after the funeral of the late sovereign to signify the rebirth of national life.

Like many facets of British life the coronation rite has evolved slowly; to some degree each age has imposed its imprint on its pageantry. To understand it one must first recall pagan England, then the arrival of the Christian message. In those primitive times the new King took office by sitting on a ceremonial stone: perhaps, it has been suggested, the tomb of his predecessor. Certainly he would have wished to be in tune with the departed spirit – and more so if his forerunner had been noted for wisdom and heroism. To complete this simple rite the installation was at once followed by a sumptuous feast, an occasion for liberal eating and drinking attended by the foremost men of the State.

These two cardinal ingredients formed the basis of the coronation right up to the last century. They even prevail in modern times, though they are now less sharply defined. From the days of the Norman William the Conqueror until 1831 the most eminent peers placed the new sovereign in a stone chair set on the 'King's Bench' in Westminster Hall. The reason for this setting was because it constituted part of the royal Palace of Westminster, the seat of government when the monarch and his Court resided in London. But Westminster was not always chosen. Indeed, the first known coronation, that of the Saxon King Edgar, was solemnized at Bath (and its one thousandth anniversary in 1973 was to be observed in the reign of Elizabeth II).

With the acceptance in England of the Christian faith, religion crept into the ritual. Bearing the Crown and other insignia high in the full gaze of the crowds, the clergy accompanied the monarch and his secular peers to Westminster Abbey near by. There he besought God for blessing and guidance during the new reign. Finally everyone returned to Westminster Hall to partake of the banquet.

True to his reputation the wastrel George IV showered such costly vulgarity on this last phase of the proceedings – much to the anger of impoverished subjects – that the next sovereign William IV removed Westminster Hall from the coronation scene. That decision has prevailed ever since.

The coronation of Queen Elizabeth II on 2 June 1953 offered the ideal chance to revert to this ancient procedure. This was thwarted however, by those officials who foolishly upheld 'tradition' when in fact it was no more than a relatively recent custom. Instead they preferred to waste public money assembling an ugly annexe (which was utterly out of keeping with the abbey's western approach) rather than let the Queen meet the magnates in the nation's most historic building, Westminster Hall.

But much was to happen before that day of excitement and rejoicing. In the early stages the preparations were fraught with muddle and bad judgement. Three months after the Queen's accession the coronation executive committee held its first meeting at St James's Palace. Twenty in number, its elderly members represented the establishment hierarchy, embracing such august figures as the Archbishop of Canterbury and the Lord Chamberlain. Their choice of 2 June was based on nothing more than a date roughly midway between the coronation of King George VI (12 May) and King George V (22 June). It seems that commercial interests were never consulted – an omission which at once sparked off protest from hoteliers and the tourist industry.

What was even more inflammatory was the decision to ban the coronation from the television screen. Millions of people not only in Britain but abroad were anxious to witness one of the greatest spectacles in the world. The committee deemed otherwise; it would be seen by only the privileged few. Fortunately this act of snobbery aroused protest. Why, it was contended, should the mass of the Queen's subjects be denied that feeling of kinship which the broadcasting of royal events intensified? There could be no sane argument against this view. The Queen's coronation was her public avowal before God dedicating her life *to the service of her people*. That meant not merely the chosen few, but all her subjects from the titled and the affluent down to the humblest person in the land.

Among the protesting voices eighty Members of Parliament tabled a motion vehemently condemning the ban. An astonishing fact then came to light: for four months after leaving the Court a report of the committee's decision had wandered from one government department to another, yet at no time had anyone questioned its wisdom. Although Winston Churchill and eight Cabinet Ministers were members of the committee, not one would accept responsibility for the decision. Clement Attlee at least confessed to having seen it, but the significance of the wording had eluded him. It was curious that Churchill and Attlee should display such ignorance considering that they both belonged to the bigger Coronation Commission of which Prince Philip was chairman.

As if to annoy the public further the committee proposed to shorten the route of the coronation drive far more drastically than that for George VI. Thus even the numbers of sightseers in the street would be reduced. Not that the Queen herself was at fault. In the end, due to her insistence, the route was greatly extended; indeed, it was one of the longest in coronation history. The Queen, moreover, over-ruled the recommendation to delete parts of the arduous three-hour ceremony.

However, the television argument was not settled so speedily. Both Churchill and the Archbishop continued to oppose; they feared that with the intrusion of cameras the ceremony might lose both its dignity and religious flavour and be reduced to nothing more than a cheap theatrical spectacle. Their concession to allow the televising of the procession west of the abbey screen only met with the public's stubborn

E

resistance. Finally the Queen herself removed the impasse. Wisely she valued the powerful link which would bind the monarchy more closely with the people. All obstacles were swept aside when she arranged a luncheon meeting at Buckingham Palace between Archbishop Fisher and BBC producers.

That was only one of a rash of problems. The burden of resolving them was invariably entrusted to the Duke of Norfolk, functioning from a house in Belgrave Square. Receiving £10 each half-year for his services as hereditary Earl Marshal, he and his ancestors had been factotums of all coronations for the past five centuries. In his twenties the Duke had supervised the coronation of George VI. But that had been sixteen years ago, and the Queen had her own marked views about the details of her coronation.

There had been, for instance, speculation as to the precedence of Prince Philip. Should he ride on horseback beside her or in a separate coach? Suggestions were swept aside when the Queen clearly outlined her husband's role. Not only would he accompany her in the state coach, but, as the foremost royal duke, he would be the first to kneel before her bareheaded in homage. He would, furthermore, participate with her in the sacrament of Holy Communion.

With her customary thoroughness, the Queen studied the Royal Library's records of earlier coronations so that the Dean of Westminster, whose privilege it was to guide the Queen in the 'solemnities and meaning' of her coronation, was surprised to find that she needed little instruction. Indeed, the Queen quickly imposed her views on the preparations. Nothing which symbolized the significance of centuries-old pageantry was allowed to be suppressed and much was revived. Thus old armils (or bracelets), emblems of wisdom and sincerity which had been ignored since the crowning of Edward VI, were restored.

Even the coronation chair in Westminster Abbey caught the Queen's critical eye. Coats of crude varnish were removed, exposing what remained of the colourful paint, gilding and enamel applied in the days of Edward I.

In the Royal Mews the State coach (built in 1762 for George
III) had already come under close scrutiny. Two years earlier
experts had been asked by George VI to inspect the decorative
carriage and had found it in a deplorable condition. The seven
famous Cipriani panels which were cracked were skilfully
removed with the aid of a surgeon's scalpel and remounted.
The coach's lining of quilted satin (which had not been renewed
since Victoria's crowning) was refurbished and lighting,
operated from batteries secreted beneath the seats was
installed. The old iron wheels, too twisted to repair, were
replaced with tyres of solid rubber to minimize jolting.
Another innovation was the concealed brackets to bear the
weight of the orb and sceptre on the route from the abbey.
Work on the coach was still in progress when the Queen's
coronation drew near.

To effect economies many of the royal coaches had been sold
soon after the war. Some had been purchased by a film
company who now happily loaned five two-pair broughams
and two open landaus – a business-like move seeing that the
vehicles were later advertised for sale in Hollywood 'as bor-
rowed by the Crown for the Coronation'.

An air of feverish activity swept the Palace to the extent that
the Queen and Prince Philip temporarily took refuge in
Windsor Castle. The State Room needed to be painted and the
carpets and curtains refurbished. In the Gold Pantry down in
the basement the celebrated gold plate came out of its glass-
fronted cases for cleaning; some items were so heavy that four
men were required to lift them. For the first time in years the
scarlet and gold State liveries were taken from steel containers.
Luckily steel and protective mothballs had served well; only the
pink silk stockings had perished.

The months that heralded the Queen's crowning were not
without amusement. A glut of claims, many of them eccentric,
sought the right to fulfil particular duties at the enthronement.
The merits or demerits of these alleged prerogatives were
debated in the Court of Claims. The Court was held traditionally in the Privy Council premises in Downing Street, and

during the past seven centuries this discreet body had assembled before each coronation to assess the validity of the various claims.

Such medieval duties as those of herb-strewers and wayfarers were summarily disposed of by a ruling automatically banning claims which had been disqualified in 1936. Therefore anyone whose claim had been allowed at the last coronation merely had to confirm this in writing.

Even so anomalies cropped up. Notable was the genuine right of the Duke of Newcastle whose claim was over-ruled on technical grounds. Traditionally, as Lord of the Manor of Worksop, it was his privilege to place the decorative white kid glove on the Queen's hand which would hold the sceptre. This simple ceremony, a brief prelude to the actual coronation, had been fulfilled by earlier ancestors at the crowning of Edward VII, George V and George VI. But times had changed; a limited company now controlled the Duke's estates, a development which gave rise to a curious situation. For the first time in the centuries-old story of the coronation, a company – the London and Fort George Land Company – attempted to take part. It was seriously suggested that while a director held Elizabeth's arm the chairman should offer the glove (which, incidentally, was lined with white silk and bore the royal cipher and embroidered rose, thistle and shamrock). Not surprisingly the law lords soon quashed the Newcastles' ancient privilege.

Roughly half a year's detailed planning took about the same amount of time to put into effect. And on the eve of the coronation itself workmen were still frantically striving to complete their respective tasks. The young Queen's determination to have a procession composed only of coaches and horses presented George Hopkins, Superintendent of the Royal Mews, with a ticklish problem. Not only had most of the coaches vanished, but also the horses with their coachmen and postilions. The snag was removed by recruiting members of the Coaching Club and borrowing horses from a London brewery firm and the army.

Despite the panic and confusion little was overlooked,

although some days before the ceremony Miss Margaret MacDonald, the ever-watchful Bobo, noticed that the abbey's robing rooms lacked mirrors. A mere two days were left to make and fit sixteen specially designed mirrors, the last being fitted only hours before the Queen's arrival.

A worse cause for alarm was the ingredients of the oil used in the anointing, the most solemn act of the crowning. Ever since biblical times the consecration of kings and queens with oil has been the moment of supreme spiritual significance. But for some hectic days it seemed that the crowning of Elizabeth II would be deprived of the sacred oil. More than a hundred years ago a quantity of the honey-coloured oil had been blended for Queen Victoria, then used at every coronation up to that of the Queen's father. Then the last phial had vanished, irretrievably lost among the debris when Nazi bombs fell on the abbey in 1941.

Aggravating the problem was the vexing discovery that the Victorian firm which owned the prescription no longer functioned. Momentarily, however, hopes ran high when an elderly household officer recalled that the Queen's father had kept a little of the precious oil as a memento; but exhaustive searches both at Buckingham Palace and Windsor Castle proved abortive. More inquiries yielded the names of the two pharmacists who had compounded the oil for the Queen's father. One had moved to Toronto but both were now dead. Yet luckily the firm that they had founded still survived; moreover the new owners had retained the formula which, dating from the time of Charles II, included 'pure myrrh one ounce, of sweet cinnamon half as much ...' as well as a rare blend of rose, musk, orange flowers, civet, ambergris, jasmine, sweet calamus and flowers of benzoin. Regrettably a piece of information was still missing: the basic oil to be used was unknown.

There was no alternative but to engage in an extensive system of detection, tracking down the relations of the one-time royal chemists, Squire and Sons. From widespread inquiries emerged enlightening news: a director had included among his mementoes a small quantity of the oil which had once been exhibited in a chemist's shop. This produced another clue, and led to the discovery of the phial in the possession of an elderly lady living near Lingfield in Surrey.

Altogether there were four ounces of this rare base dating back to Victoria's reign. Two ounces were consecrated anew for Queen Elizabeth, and the remainder has been stored safely for the coronation of her heir apparent.

As her coronation loomed nearer the Queen carefully rehearsed the detailed ceremonial. On 1 May there began at Buckingham Palace a number of rehearsals in the White Drawing Room (at one time the music room of Queen Victoria's consort). White tapes marked out the precise dimensions of the theatre – that area in the abbey where the coronation takes place – and by playing records of her father's coronation on a radiogram she worked out each stage of the ceremony. One of the most exacting aspects was the judging of distances while moving from point to point to synchronize with the different phases of the ritual.

To assess the steps needed from the abbey's West Door to the Theatre rehearsals were transferred to the more spacious State Ballroom. Again accurate measurements were taken, and the timing of the Queen's procession was gauged almost to the last second. Indeed the timing throughout the coronation reached such perfection that the Earl Marshal was able to announce in advance that Queen Elizabeth would be crowned 'at about 12.34'. In actual fact the Archbishop of Canterbury placed Saint Edward's Crown on the Queen's head at 12.33 and thirty seconds.

One problem was the manoeuvring of the enormous sixty-foot train of the coronation robe. To overcome this the Queen, accompanied by her six maids of honour, practised with a long white sheet trailing from her shoulders. For the moment large gold and white chairs served as an improvised coach, and with these she went through the motions of ascending and descending.

Some weeks before the coronation the Imperial State Crown had to be moved from the security of the Tower of London so that it could be altered to fit the Queen's head. In an age when robbery was rife precautions for its safety gave some concern. Finally the authorities relied on a simple ruse. Concealed in a hat-box it was conveyed to the Palace in a private car, escorted by men who gave no indication that they were military marksmen. The plain clothes officers in an accompanying police car possessed nothing more lethal than truncheons.

On the eve of the coronation, the rest of the regalia was moved from the Tower to the Abbey's Jerusalem Chamber. There, traditionally, it was protected by the Yeomen of the Guard. Unknown to the public the fabulous Crown Jewels had travelled through the streets of London in a tarpaulin-covered van, while replicas in their leather cases were conveyed quite normally by the police.

The coronation regalia as seen today originated in the reign of Charles II. In September 1940, when a Nazi invasion of Britain seemed imminent, the regalia was stored for safety at Windsor Castle. Other than that for seven centuries it has been secure in the Jewel House in the Tower. The world's most celebrated collection of jewels has been assessed at twenty million pounds. But no one can give an accurate figure, and to the people of Britain it is priceless.

The story of the regalia goes back at least to the far-off Saxon days of Edward the Confessor. Fascinatingly the Queen's crowning was an 'echo' over the centuries of Edward's coronation in 1043. His Great Seal depicts him on his throne, crowned, an orb in one hand, a sceptre surmounted by a cross in the other. On the reverse side, one hand grasps a staff with a dove; there is a sword in the other. Tradition also asserts that he wore a ring. To this extent, therefore, the rudiments of the coronation were common to both the crowning of the sainted Edward and Elizabeth II. The sole exception were the spurs, the emblems of knighthood which crept into the ritual when chivalry arrived in the twelfth century.

Apparently by the mid-thirteenth century in the reign of Henry III two sets of regalia were in being: St Edward's which was used solely at coronations and was in the care of the monks of Westminster Abbey; and the royal regalia which was kept in the Tower. It was still there when the Civil War broke out in 1642 between the Royalists of Charles 1 and the Parliamentary Roundheads. Wishing to rid the State of monarchic symbols the Parliamentarians ordered Sir Henry Mildmay, Keeper of the Jewel House, to hand over the treasure in his custody. Being a Cromwellian supporter Mildmay obediently complied, a sycophantic act which earned him the despicable title of 'Knave of Diamonds'. Of sterner stuff, the Dean and Chapter of Westminster Abbey defiantly locked their regalia out of sight, only yielding when Charles 1 died on the scaffold.

Loathing anything identified with the dead monarch, Parliament had the regalia broken up, melted down or sold. Luckily, through the loyalty and ingenuity of the Westminster priests, two coronation treasures happily escaped this vandalism: the silver-gilt Romanesque anointing spoon and the gilt eagle-shaped ampulla of fine gold which holds the oil. Jewels from the crowns also disappeared in the sales, but it is thought that some were reacquired by zealous Royalists. At least some reappeared in the new regalia made in 1661 by Sir Robert Vyner, the royal goldsmith, for Charles 11's coronation. Most of the gold had been sent to the Royal Mint for coining, but it is possible that fragments survived and were used by Vyner.

Among the survivors also was the huge ruby given, so tradition claims, to the Black Prince by Pedro the Cruel, King of Castile, after the Prince's success in 1307 at the Battle of Najera. The original owner was the King of Granada whom Pedro reputedly murdered for his jewels. This famous gem is most probably the 'rock ruby' bought by a 'Mr Cooke' for fifteen pounds at the time of the Commonwealth. Possibly the Black Prince wore it on his helmet in battle, but there is no doubt that it appeared in the coronet that encircled the helmet of Henry v at the Battle of Agincourt in 1415. Another relic was the sapphire from the ring of Edward the Confessor.

Both these romantic stones were set in the Imperial State crown which was made in 1838 for the coronation of Queen

Victoria and was worn by Queen Elizabeth after her crowning. Indeed since the time of Queen Mary II the magnificent ruby has predominated in the State crown.

A delightful story relates to the ancient sapphire. Legend claims that Edward the Confessor wore it in a ring and while he was proceeding to a shrine dedicated to St John the Evangelist a vagrant appeared begging for alms. Because he had already distributed his money Edward could offer nothing but the ring. Years later towards the end of his reign two pilgrims returned the ring to him at his palace at Havering in Essex. They did so, they said, at the request of an old man in the East who, claiming to be St John, had been the beggar who had once confronted the King. There was a further message: that he and Edward would meet in Paradise. It is said that the King still wore the ring at his burial some months later. Like all her ancestors, Queen Elizabeth wore a coronation ring to symbolize this honoured relic.

History records that when in the twelfth century St Edward's tomb was opened in Westminster Abbey, the ring was taken away by Abbot Lawrence. Whether or not it was presented to the reigning monarch or retained by the abbey is not certain. But it is possible that it was the sapphire which James Guinon acquired for sixty pounds during Cromwell's rule.

Apart from these stones the Imperial State Crown contains over three thousand diamonds, 277 pearls, seventeen sapphires, eleven emeralds and four rubies. One big gem is the Stuart sapphire which may have been the stone confiscated by Edward IV after George Neville, Archbishop of York, had worn it in his mitre. It was incorporated in the state crown of Charles II, whose brother James II carried it on his person in exile. On his death it passed to James' son, the Old Pretender, then to the latter's younger son, Henry Benedict, Cardinal York, the last of the Stuarts. In 1807, shortly before his death, the cardinal, who had worn the sapphire in his mitre, sold it to a Viennese merchant. It returned to England when it was bought for the Prince Regent, subsequently George IV.

Though there is no proof the crown's four drop-shaped pearls are traditionally said to have been worn by Elizabeth I as ear-rings. But a portrait in the National Portrait Gallery in London shows that they are more likely to have been the ear-rings of James I's daughter, Elizabeth, Princess Palatine and Queen of Bohemia. After the Restoration she returned to England where she died. Thus they may have again been included in the Crown Jewels or Elizabeth may have presented them to her renowned daughter Sophia, Electress of Hanover, the mother of George I. The tradition persists that the original owner was Mary Queen of Scots who, while imprisoned in Lochleven Castle, was dispossessed of her jewels. Some of these, among them pearls of rare beauty, were bought by Elizabeth I for twelve thousand crowns.

The crown which really grips the imagination is that named after Edward the Confessor. The original, a Saxon diadem 'of gould wyerworke sett with slight stones and two little bells', was a victim of Cromwell's vandalism. But for the stupidity of the Parliamentary Commissioners, Elizabeth II might have been crowned with one of England's greatest relics, for it is thought that this was also the crown of Alfred the Great. Only the name lingers on in the crown used at the Queen's coronation. Yet there is an intriguing possibility that when Sir Robert Vyner produced the new St Edward's Crown for Charles II he used a crown which had been part of the regalia of the Lord Protector. Rather hypocritically Oliver Cromwell possessed a crown. In 1656 he is thought to have been offered the throne but to have declined it. Yet a crown, orb and sceptre were displayed at his funeral two years later, and then with his effigy in Westminster Abbey until the effigy was hung contemptuously from a window of the Jewel House in Whitehall at the Restoration. There is speculation that this was the crown that Vyner redesigned. If that is so the crown placed on the head of Queen Elizabeth II belongs, in effect, to the old regalia, but no one knows if it was originally the state crown of Henry VIII – which set the pattern of English crowns as we know them – or if it was a considerably older one, such as the 'German crown' which, remodelled for Richard II, was worn by the maligned King John.

One large gem in the regalia is indisputably authentic: the Cullinan diamond. In 1905 Frederick Wells, manager of De Beers' Premier mine in South Africa, gouged from the rocks with his walking stick what at first he took to be a piece of crystal. Then dashing into the office of Sir Thomas Cullinan, the company's president, he said excitedly: 'Look at what I've found!' Sir Thomas, barely glancing up from his writing replied: 'Wells, either that is the largest diamond in the world or you are fired!'

The diamond (christened after Cullinan) weighed the fantastic amount of 3,106 carats. Two years later the Transvaal Government presented it to Edward VII as a birthday gift, requesting that it should be set in the English crown. But in its original state it was much too big and the King instructed that it should be split. J. Asscher of Amsterdam was commissioned for this delicate assignment. But so acute was the strain that as he delivered the critical blow he fainted. On regaining consciousness he swooned again when he saw how perfect had been his skill. In due course the two pieces were split again and thus came into being the Four Stars of Africa. The largest, believed to be the biggest cut diamond in the world, now graces the royal sceptre with the cross (the symbol of kingly power and justice). The second star glitters in the Imperial State Crown and the third and fourth were set in the crown of Queen Mary for the coronation of King George V. Called the Lesser Stones of Africa these gems are cleverly mounted so that they can be removed and worn independently as brooch or pendant. Though the rest of the regalia belongs to the State these two excellent diamonds are owned by the Queen, who refers to them as 'Granny's chips'.

The other main items of the coronation regalia include the jewelled state sword (the sovereign's personal sword), the golden spurs (symbolizing knightly chivalry), the golden orb surmounted by its jewelled cross (signifying the monarch's obedience to the Christian faith) and the sceptre with the dove (denoting equity and mercy).

At her coronation the Queen deliberately avoided the pitfalls which almost marred her father's ceremony. For the crowning of George VI red thread had indicated the back from the front of St Edward's Crown. But it was so indistinct that the Archbishop had almost placed the crown the wrong way round. To prevent such a recurrence the Queen had two silver stars sewn on to guide the myopic Primate.

Gold lace was also banned from the velvet cushions on which were borne the regalia. At her father's coronation, the Garter insignia of the Marquis of Salisbury had become entangled with St Edward's Crown while he carried it and he had finally had to rip himself free. Behind him the Duke of Portland was even more embarrassed when the pendant of his Garter collar became entwined with the Queen Consort's crown. Only the speedy action of the resplendent Garter King of Arms saved an awkward moment.

For the Queen's coronation even the carpeting was specially woven. At Geoge VI's crowning the thick pile had offered such stubborn resistance to lengthy trains that some of the older peers, reduced almost to a state of collapse, had had to be carried off by ambulance.

If Queen Elizabeth adhered to the medieval ritual books she prayed throughout the night preceding her coronation. Well known for her religious beliefs maybe she did spend some time in prayer. Medieval monarchs, however, were not encumbered with the duties of a modern sovereign. Neither were their coronations a world event. The curious thing about the Queen's coronation is that it was like a magnet to other nations, even to republics. Like pilgrims to some hallowed Mecca official representatives journeyed from seventy-four foreign States and sightseers flocked from abroad in their thousands. From Australia alone came sixty thousand and from the United States despite the lingering memories of George III travelled another forty thousand, among them 850 who were happy to pay £160,000 for a ten-day jamboree. If the cynics argued that British monarchy was on the wane there was no sign of it. Anyone with a view along the five-mile route could turn it into gold: sixty-five pounds for a seat in Park Lane and for a street balcony with champagne for fifty, a staggering three and a half thousand. To catch a glimpse of the radiant young Queen half-a-million people stoically endured London's peevish climate and camped for forty-eight hours on the street pavements.

Forty-three thousand troops arrived from overseas and massive grandstands, richly decked with flowers and bunting, bore the strain of 110,000 people. Into the Abbey itself the Duke of Norfolk crammed another seven thousand, granting a meagre eighteen inches per seat with an extra inch for a peer with robes.

But how different from the coronations of long ago, not only as a world spectacle but because the opening rite – the presenting of the Queen to the people – seemed to be out of keeping with modern times. If like her earlier forebears Elizabeth II had been enthroned in the Parliamentary environment of Westminster Hall, it would have been closer to its original purpose; for Parliament, especially the House of Commons which represents the people, has inherited the powers of the medieval peers who once raised the monarch to the stone chair on the King's Bench. When it is recalled that Queen Elizabeth II, as in the case of all the heirs generals of Sophia of Hanover, sits on the throne by virtue of the Parliamentary Act of Settlement of 1701 her appearance before the people's representatives would have been more apt. As it was all this had to be taken for granted when the Archbishop of Canterbury, the first subject in the land, called on the assembled gathering in the abbey to accept the Queen by acclamation.

Swearing the threefold oath: to govern her people according to their respective laws, to ensure law and justice in all her judgements, and to preserve the Protestant religion in the United Kingdom, the Queen was continuing an ancient practice which certainly dated back to the year 973. To an appreciable extent it gave birth to constitutional government and limited monarchy for Magna Carta, the Great Charter which guaranteed England (and indeed many other parts of the world where Britain once ruled) national liberties was an intricate development of the coronation oath of the Plantagenet sovereigns. On Monday 15 June 1215, on the little island of Runnymede in the Thames near Windsor, an uncompromising coalition of churchmen and barons had forced King John to seal the Charter. John had infringed the liberties of the Church, the barons, cities and boroughs. By imposing arbitrary taxes he had broken the law. Angrily gnawing sticks and straw – the floor covering of these times – tradition asserts that John cried : 'They have given me five-and-twenty over-kings.' But the Charter became the most powerful instrument in advancing democracy. In that respect Magna Carta was the fount of constitutional government or government according to the law.

Thus the coronation oath – the prelude to the actual crowning – was a declaration that, because all authority is said to emanate from the Queen, all authority in her domain comes within the control of the law. Even the service of Holy Communion in which the crowning itself was dovetailed was an expression that, as one writer has fittingly claimed, 'everything done to her or by her in the rite was to be understood as having relation to the peoples of whom she is the representative'.

The coronation's most sacred and mystical act was the anointing : a rite symbolizing divine confirmation of the people's choice. (This Frankish ceremony was first recorded in England in AD 785 when Offa, the King of Mercia, had his son Egfrith anointed and crowned as his successor : the first known Christian consecration, incidentally, of an Anglo-Saxon monarch). For this ritual the Queen sat in King Edward's chair in which is ensconced the legendary Stone of Scone, reputed to have been Jacob's pillow at Bethel, on which Scottish kings were crowned. As it was feared that Scottish Nationalists would steal it the Stone had been secreted beneath a flagstone in the abbey vaults. On the night before the coronation detectives attended its removal with block and tackle to where it truly belonged.

When the Archbishop anointed the Queen on the head, breast and hands, 'as kings, priests and prophets were anointed, and as Solomon was anointed king by Zadok the priest and Nathan the prophet', it gave her claim to the royal title. Years ago, until this stage of the ceremony, her rank would have been Duchess of Edinburgh and no more.

In olden times an anointed monarch was deemed to be endowed with the miraculous touch for scrofula. Ailing subjects would kneel to receive the sovereign's hands on their faces. As many as six hundred were known to file past Charles II in one session. The diseased placed such faith in his powers of healing that patients sometimes journeyed even from the New World. 'Touch-pieces', worn around the neck, were distributed to those who had felt the monarch's hands. Queen Anne in the eighteenth century was the last sovereign to perform this ceremony. One of the children who received her touch for the 'King's Evil' would achieve fame as Dr Samuel Johnson.

Two items in the regalia reflect the British way of life: the sceptre (the symbol of authority) received by the Queen's right hand and the rod with the dove which, placed simultaneously in her left hand, signifies that the fulfilment of the law is tempered with mercy.

Thus in a service which embraced the Teutonic, Christian and Norman-French facets of the British nation, the Queen had been dedicated almost as a sacrificial victim to the service of her God and her people. The Teutonic aspect had been witnessed in the Recognition – the acclamation of the Queen – not with the strident clash of knightly swords upon shields, but by the Queen's Scholars of Westminster School shouting: 'Vivat Regina Elizabeth! Vivat! Vivat! Vivat!' St Edward's Crown, a circle of gold and jewels, had replaced the Teutonic helmet of the tribal leader. The Christian Church had proclaimed Elizabeth II as its servant and the kneeling peers, each promising to become her 'Liege man of Life and Limb and earthly worship', had obeyed the Norman feudal rite of homage.

But the Queen's coronation did not escape its critics. It was accused of bolstering the prestige of the Reformed Church and of reaffirming the rights of the nobles in Magna Carta. One critic argued that the ceremony was more purely national and restrictive, more Anglican and medieval than ever before. Modern monarchy symbolizes a democratic way of life, yet the participants at her coronation were drawn solely from the aristocracy and the Establishment. In keeping with medieval times but somehow out of step with today the bishops and the lay lords placed the Queen on the throne, an act signifying that she is given possession of her domain. Yet ironically the Members of the House of Commons, the representatives of the nation as a whole, looked on huddled together in an upper gallery.

And although she is the Queen of several countries she was traditionally crowned not even Queen of the United Kingdom, but solely of England. The explanation for this is that the coronation is directly identified with the Church of England and only in England is this denomination established. The Queen reigns over people of other denominations yet in her oath she merely guaranteed to maintain 'the Protestant reformed Religion established by law'. At his coronation the Queen's grandfather King George v declined to sign the Protestant declaration, submitting that passages were offensive to his Roman Catholic subjects; he merely swore that he himself was a faithful Protestant.

But in spite of any shortcomings or criticisms of the Queen's coronation the people loved it.

﷼ 5 *The Supreme Governor*

At her coronation Queen Elizabeth gave her solemn avowal to 'preserve inviolably the settlement of the Church of England, and the doctrine, worship, discipline and government thereof, as by law established in England'. Briefly, she is Defender of the Faith and the Supreme Governor of the Anglican Church. Dating from Tudor times both titles were offshoots of controversy and crystallize a wealth of religious history. They pinpoint, moreover, the Queen's status in the Church, a position which is confusing to many.

When Martin Luther ranted loudly in Europe against corruption in the Catholic Church, Henry VIII, hurrying to the defence of Rome, answered the turbulent German monk with a cogent book on the sacraments. 'Defender of the Faith' was the grandiose title accorded the King by a grateful Pope. But then the relationship soured. Resenting papal intervention in the affairs of his kingdom, in 1530 Henry joined in the revolution against papal authority which led to the Reformation in England. With Parliament's backing four years later the Supremacy Act declared 'that the King, our sovereign lord, his heirs and successors, Kings of this realm, shall be taken, accepted and reputed the only supreme head on earth of the Church of England'. But Henry desired to rule the Church not in a spiritual but in a secular sense. Neither did he necessarily wish to lift the English Church out of the Catholic sphere. Yet this was inescapable, partly due to conflicting religious allegiances among the Tudors themselves.

Edward VI, Henry's sickly son and heir, was a Protestant. But even if he had wished to champion Catholic practice, as a ten-

F

year-old boy he could scarcely have resisted the powerful political force which greedily wanted to enrich itself with the wealth of the Church. Henry had himself unleashed this wave of avarice by suppressing the monastries, then selling both property and lands to restock his coffers. Thus in Edward's reign the Church of England swung completely over to Protestantism.

In 1553 when Edward died of 'a tough, strong, straining cough', the religious scene changed again. This was to be expected for Edward was succeeded by his half-sister Mary, named 'Bloody Mary' from her burning of heretics at London's Smithfield and elsewhere in a desperate, fanatical bid to reinject England with the Catholic doctrine. One can only speculate on what the situation would be today had not illness removed her after a five-year reign. One thing is quite certain: Queen Elizabeth II would never have sat on the throne.

Not much is known about the true religious sentiments of the first Elizabeth, the half-sister who followed Mary. Whatever they happened to be she was tolerant and did not wish 'to make windows into men's souls'. Perhaps political rather than religious motives guided the actions of this astute monarch. Inheriting a kingdom torn by religious strife, she restored a reasonable semblance of order with the Act of Supremacy, declaring herself to be 'the only supreme governor of the realm ... as well in all spiritual or ecclesiastical matters as in temporal'. Thus she bequeathed the title of Supreme Governor to all her successors.

James I, the next sovereign, allowed the middle-course English Church to go undisturbed simply because he hated religious extremists. He never forgot that the Puritanical element in Scotland had dubbed him 'God's silly vassal', and he spurned Catholicism just as much. The only change he approved was the Authorized Version of the Bible. The Church of England that existed at his death endeared itself so profoundly to his son that the God-fearing Charles I was willing to die for it.

During the decade of the Commonwealth Parliament, and

most of the English, were steeped in Protestantism and meant to stay that way. Thus at the Restoration Charles II who had decided Catholic leanings had enough wisdom to keep them secret. Not so his less discreet brother. Even before his accession as James II he overtly supported the Catholic cause.

For a while a mainly Protestant England tolerated him, imagining that on his death his Protestant daughter Mary, the wife of William of Orange, would succeed him. But there was the unexpected birth of a son, an event which fired the tinder of revolution in England. When William and Mary were invited to share the throne Parliament made certain, once and for all, to rid England of Catholic kings. By the Act of Settlement of 1701 the politicians wrote the union between Protestant Church and Protestant monarch into the law of England.

Henceforth no Roman Catholic prince could wear the Crown; neither could the heir marry a Roman Catholic. To make certain of this the monarch would swear it in the coronation oath. Thus after the death of Queen Anne, Parliament baulked Catholic Stuart claims to the throne and brought the Protestant Hanoverians to England.

That is one reason why Elizabeth II reigns today. Her status is defined in the Act of Settlement which affirms that anyone 'who shall ... profess the Popish religion, or marry a Papist, should be excluded and forever incapable to inherit, possess or enjoy the Crown and government of this Realm and Ireland, and the Dominions thereunto belonging, or any part of the same, or to have, use, or exercise any Regal Power, authority or jurisdiction within the same. . . .'

The Queen must necessarily be a communicant member of the Church of England. As Princess Elizabeth she was confirmed on Saturday 28 March 1942 at Windsor – the final duty of Cosmo Gordon Lang before retiring as Archbishop of Canterbury.

I had always hoped [he entered in his diary] that I might have this privilege. The night before I had spent at the Castle and

73

had a full talk with the little lady alone. She had been prepared by Stafford Crawley at Windsor, and though naturally not very communicative, she showed real intelligence and understanding. I thought much, but rightly said little of the responsibility which may be waiting her in the future – this future more than ever unknown. The Confirmation was very simple – the ugly private chapel at the Castle – only a few relatives and friends and the boys of St George's choir present – my address was just as I have so often given in country churches.

Although Prince Philip the Queen's consort is forbidden to belong to the Church of Rome, he is not compelled to be a member of the Anglican Church. In fact he did leave the Greek Orthodox Church to join the Church of England.

As secular head of the Established Church the Queen appoints the two archbishops, and the bishops, on the Prime Minister's recommendation. But if she had any pronounced views doubtless these would be considered.

Before his enthronement a bishop must visit the Queen to make his homage – a ceremony usually held at Buckingham Palace. Ushered into the Queen's presence by the Master of the Household, the bishop in his robes is accompanied by the Clerk of the Closet (himself a bishop), who is in charge of the Queen's Ecclesiastical Household. Kneeling before Her Majesty and placing his hands between hers as a sign of loyalty, the new prelate repeats after the Secretary of State for Home Affairs: 'I acknowledge that I hold the said bishopric, as well as the spiritualities as the temporalities thereof only of Your Majesty and for these temporalities I personally give my homage to Your Majesty.'

Because the Queen is the *secular* head of the Church the bishop pays homage for the temporalities, not the spiritualities. His consecration is solely a matter for the Church, but it is from the Queen that he is granted the right to fulfil his duties in his diocese. A bishop who is promoted to archbishop makes homage once more as do all bishops to move to another see.

Indeed the Queen appoints all the leading hierarchy of the Church, and the Judicial Committee of Her Majesty's Privy Council is the Church's Court of Appeal in all ecclesiastical affairs.

A candidate for a bishopric is chosen according to a certain procedure. The Dean and Chapter seek the Queen's approval (after first consulting the Prime Minister) to fill the vacancy. Next the Prime Minister (after discussions with the Archbishop of Canterbury and maybe the Archbishop of York) submits the name of a candidate to the Queen. A licence – a *congé d'élire* – together with a Letter Missive (containing the nominee's name), is now submitted to the Dean and Chapter to complete the election. For this august body to refuse could incur the forfeiture of lands, goods and chattels, the loss of sovereign rights and imprisonment 'during Royal pleasure' under the Statute of Praemunire.

It is very unfortunate that if the Dean and Chapter resent their proposed bishop they can do nothing but accept. Dr Samuel Johnson summed up a truism when it was argued that a *congé d'élire* lacked power of enforcement. He replied: 'Sir, it is such a recommendation as if I should throw you out of a two pair of stairs window and recommend you to fall to the ground.' At times of dissention a sharp letter from the Prime Minister has sufficed to bring a recalcitrant Dean to heel.

As a rule the new bishop is legally confirmed at the Court of Arches in the presence of representatives of the Crown. The Dean of the Court reads the Letters Patent and the Queen's seal is on view. It is at the next stage that the bishop makes his homage. Finally comes the enthronement.

Queen Elizabeth appoints a bishop but is not empowered to dismiss him. At first sight this is yet another English idiosyncrasy, but the explanation is simple. Up to the Reformation the right to dismiss was vested solely in the Pope. Afterwards that power was inherited by the sovereign, but it vanished over the course of time. However, as the Supreme Governor of the Established Church, the Queen retains the right to receive the resignation of an archbishop.

As already explained the senior cleric in the Queen's Ecclesiastical Household is the Clerk of the Closet. In his centuries-old office he controls the College of Chaplains which includes the Deputy Clerk and thirty-six chaplains. In the main their duties are of an honorary nature, among them preaching in the Chapels Royal at the Tower of London, Hampton Court, St James's Palace, Windsor (where the Queen and her family invariably worship on Sunday mornings) and elsewhere.

All the churches directly connected with the sovereign bear the curious name of 'Royal Peculiars'. What is more surprising all are aloof from the dictates of the archbishops or even the bishops in whose dioceses they happen to be. The most prominent is Westminster Abbey – the Collegiate Church of St Peter – where not even the Bishop of London can trespass on the affairs of the Dean and Chapter. The Queen, who is known as the 'Visitor', is the fount of authority.

Another Royal Peculiar of distinction is the Queen's Chapel of the Savoy, her own attractive shrine as the Duke of Lancaster. Today used by the Royal Victorian Order the chapel was added, along with the rest of the property of the House of Lancaster, to Crown possessions by Henry IV. The royal palace has long since disappeared and a famous hotel looms high on its site. But the valuable land on which it soars is that of the Lord of the Manor of Savoy who is the Queen.

To Queen Elizabeth religion is not a formality. She is deeply religious and has been inspired by the example of her devout father; her convictions sustain her in her manifold duties. When at Windsor (which is mostly at weekends), the royal family worship at a modest little chapel in the heart of the Great Park. At Sandringham they attend the old parish church and when residing at Holyroodhouse in Edinburgh they go to St Giles' Cathedral. During the summer vacation at Balmoral the royal place of worship is the hillside Presbyterian Church of Craithie, a few miles from the castle. On her travels abroad the Queen visits the local Anglican church. In northern Europe these come within the jurisdiction of the Bishop of Fulham who invariably accompanies the sovereign if she visits one.

Since Victoria's reign Queen Elizabeth's predecessors have reacted to religion in their own particular way. So engrossed was the Queen's great-great-grandmother in Church affairs that, in the appointments to high office, she carefully studied the candidate's qualities and suitability for the environment in which he would function. More than once she exercised her veto in the appointment of a bishop. Queen Victoria's conception of religion was essentially a simple one. At Windsor only bishops could wear all their robes; other clerics had to make do with a cassock. Suspicious of change, for a long time she opposed the introduction of *Hymns Ancient and Modern*. Anyone preaching at Windsor had a critical listener in the Queen, who expected the text of the sermon and the hymns to be sung to await her in her private pew.

Her son Edward VII never embroiled himself in religious matters, provided that priests never wore moustaches. Not so her grandson George V. Reading his Bible daily he was so sensitive to the religious sensibilities of others that after his accession he refused to open Parliament unless the Parliamentary Declaration was stripped of its seventeenth-century anti-Catholic bigotry. Parliament had introduced this declaration, delivered by the monarch 'on the day of the meeting of the first Parliament after his accession', by an Act of 1678 'for the more effectual preserving of the King's person and Government by disabling Papists from sitting in either House of Commons'.

The Queen's father, whose favourite hymns were the ones he had sung lustily in the choir at the naval base at Portsmouth, was equally broadminded. As head of State he endeavoured in a practical way to stimulate the acceptance of the Christian faith as an essential part of the pattern of life.

Because of her genuine interest in the Church it was appropriate that the first public function of Queen Elizabeth's reign was the annual Royal Maundy ceremony. Introduced into England by Edward I in the thirteenth century the name is derived from *mandatum* (commandment) and relates to Christ's washing of his disciples' feet at the Last Supper. For that reason it is observed on the Thursday before Easter.

In the reign of the first Elizabeth a series of officials, graduating in rank, cleansed the feet of the poor before they reached the sovereign who then applied scented water and towels. Intended to be a public expression of humility, this observance was maintained by English monarchs until James II. Royal participation was revived by King George v in 1932.

Today recipients – one-time householders and ratepayers – receive Maundy Money, in other days the dress worn at the ceremony by the Queen was presented to the oldest woman. Minted specially for the event Maundy coins are of silver and comprise the penny, the half groat or twopenny, the three-penny and the groat or fourpenny piece. The penny was the Norman *sterling* (so christened because it bore a star) from which the British derived the name of their currency. Originally 240 sterlings weighed one pound. That is why, until decimalization, 240 pennies were equal to one pound sterling. Maundy currency is presented to an equal number of old men and women totalling the monarch's age. For years it was customary to distribute the cash gift in Westminster Abbey, but each year the Queen has tended to change the setting. When she visited St Albans Cathedral in 1957 it was the first time a sovereign had not presented Maundy money out of London since the days of the Merry Monarch, Charles II.

A similar custom is now only fulfilled in the Queen's name. This occurs on 6 January, the Feast of the Epiphany, when gold (twenty-five sovereigns), frankincense and myrrh are presented on gold salvers on the Queen's orders to symbolize the offerings of the Three Kings at the Nativity. Not since George II has a sovereign attended in person. Instead two Gentlemen Ushers from her household, attended by the colourful Yeomen of the Guard, deputize for Her Majesty at St James's Palace.

North of the border Queen Elzabeth's link with the Established Church of Scotland is more frail than that with its English counterpart. And yet at her Accession Council the only official documents that she signed related to her willingness to preserve the Presbyterian government of the Church of Scotland.

After recognizing that the Queen is the source of all secular authority the Church displays an independent spirit which is apparent in its fourth Declaratory Article: 'The Church is part of the Universal Church wherein the Lord Jesus Christ has appointed a government in the hands of church office-bearers. It receives from Him, its Divine King and Head, and from Him alone, the right and power, subject to no civil authority, to legislate and adjudicate finally in all matters of doctrine, worship, government and discipline in the Church.'

Each year when the General Assembly of Ministers and Elders of the Church of Scotland convenes in Edinburgh to debate its affairs the Queen is represented by a Lord High Commissioner (usually a distinguished member of the Church). He is there not to preside but, as one Commissioner has described it, 'to see that the Church, whose spiritual authority she recognizes, does not trespass on to her temporalities'. While at the General Assembly the Lord High Commissioner resides at the Palace of Holyroodhouse, the only occasion when a royal palace is at the disposal of one of the Queen's officers. And this officer is honoured as if the Queen were present herself. When the assembly opens he accompanies the procession to the Assembly Hall, attended by the Lord Lyon King-of-Arms and the Purse-Bearer with mace. The gallery that he occupies is regarded as being technically outside the assembly. Later he reports the proceedings to the Queen.

Although the Queen is the protector of both the Church of England and the Church of Scotland the Archbishop of Canterbury once made it clear at a meeting of the Church Assembly that she is a 'member of one only'. This fact did not deter the headstrong Queen Victoria from taking the sacrament at Craithie – an act which stirred up the resentment of the Archbishop of Canterbury of the day. But since Victoria only once has a monarch participated in the Communion service in the

Church of Scotland. This was in 1969, by the Queen, during the General Assembly.

Doubtless the Church of England is watchful of royal behaviour. No one can deny that the shadow of the Archbishop of Canterbury fell darkly on Edward VIII during the Abdication crisis. But even in minor matters the Anglican Church is keenly observant, as was demonstrated to the Queen Mother in the autumn of 1950. The incident concerned Lady Anson, her niece, and Prince George of Denmark, who, with the consent of her brother, the Earl of Strathmore, were to be married in the private chapel at Glamis Castle. The Earl's own chaplain, a minister of the Scottish Episcopal Church, was to officiate and the Queen Mother announced her intention to attend. Unfortunately there was an aspect of the proposed union which displeased the Anglican Church: although she was the innocent party Lady Anson's first marriage had been dissolved. While it does not openly impose a ban the Church of England does not approve of the remarriage of a divorced person.

At the Archbishop's instance the Earl's chaplain withdrew – even though the Primate's authority over the Episcopal Church is virtually nil – and it was tacitly stressed that the Queen Mother should be absent from the ceremony. Rather humiliatingly the Queen Mother sat in a nearby drawing room while the marriage was solemnized, then joined the party at the subsequent luncheon.

With characteristic dignity the Queen Mother submitted to the Church. Her attitude was typical of the irreproachable standards set by the royal family today. Indeed, apart from symbolizing religious life in Britain, the Queen personifies its high morals too – a vital factor in a society which has decidedly grown more permissive. Actually the Queen's contributon to the nation's morality is immeasurable, the more so when the Established Church, non-conformity and even the Catholic Church are on the decline. Benjamin Disraeli in 1872 emphasized precisely this point, stressing that the influence of the Crown 'is not confined merely to political affairs. England is a domestic country. Here home is revered and the hearth sacred. The nation is represented by a family – the royal family – and if that family is educated with a sense of responsibility and a sentiment of public duty, it is difficult to exaggerate the salutory influence they may exercise over a nation.'

This commendable behaviour accounts for much of the monarchy's strength today. Its weakness at times in the past could be ascribed to laxity. Some of the Hanoverians, for instance, could scarcely claim to be a model of domestic rectitude or paragons of royal behaviour. Lord Mahon felt impelled to write: 'A flight of hungry Hanoverians, like so many famished vultures, fell with keen eye and bended talons on the fruitful soil of England.' Thackeray was equally scathing: 'The German women plundered, the German secretaries plundered, the German cooks and attendants plundered; even Mustapha and mahomet, the German negroes, had a share in the booty.'

And on the death of George iv a *Times* editorial ran: 'There never was an individual less regretted by his fellow creatures than the deceased King. What eye has wept for him? What heart has heaved one sob of unnecessary sorrow? ... If George iv ever had a friend – a devoted friend in any rank of life – we protest that the name of him or her never reached us. An inveterate voluptary....'

The brusque William iv was not given to debauchery and to some degree attempted to repair the self-inflicted damage to the monarchy. Yet even he was noted for his odd behaviour which prompted *The Times* to describe him as 'grotesque'. And on his death in 1837 the *Spectator* wrote: 'His late Majesty, though at times a jovial and, for a king, an honest man, was a weak. ignorant, commonplace sort of person ... William iv was to the last a popular sovereign, but his very popularity was acquired at the price of something like public contempt.'

There was a time when even Queen Victoria, that exemplar of uprightness, met with public displeasure. But this resulted mainly from her virtual retirement from public life after the Prince Consort's death. W. E. Gladstone, that political giant whom Victoria detested, wrote of the Widow of Windsor:

'We have arrived at a great crisis of royalty. The Queen is invisible; the Prince of Wales is not respected.' Even when she reappeared on the public scene to become a figure of love 'in the noblest office on earth' there were derisory voices. On 19 July 1897 one of her subjects wrote:

> Will any flunky in Christendom tell us one good thing that the Queen, her sons and daughters or any of her inexhaustible brood of pauper relations 'made in Germany' has ever done for the people of this land? ... The robbery and the jobbery, of which the Queen has been the 'heart and soul' are simply appalling. ... In fifty years she has wrung from them directly and indirectly from eighty to ninety millions sterling. She has jobbed all her children and German cousins into the highest public offices without the slightest regard to their qualifications. ...
>
> At Westminster Abbey next Tuesday, ten thousand persons ... all blasphemously falling down and worshipping a pampered old woman of sullen visage and sordid mind, because she is supposed to have in her veins some of the tainted fluid which coursed in those of that devotee of Sodom and Gomorrah, James I. Think of it, just Heavens!

One cannot conceive of reading such words about Queen Elizabeth II. Indeed the worst indictment so far was the fatuous strictures of Lord Altrincham. Yet he speedily learnt that most British people objected to ludicrous criticism of their monarch. In an unexpected appraisal of the Queen's 'defects' as the sovereign, he concluded that there was scope for improvement. Commenting that as the Queen grew older her appeal to the nation would rely less on her physical appearance and more on her personality, he argued: 'It will not then be enough to go through the motions: she will have to say things that people will remember and do things on her own initiative, which will make people sit up and take notice. As yet there is little sign that such a personality is emerging.'

The Queen had inherited from her mother an odd way of pronouncing certain words with what has been described as a 'dipthonged O'. 'The personality conveyed by the utterances which are put into her mouth,' commented Lord Altrincham, criticising her mode of speaking, 'is that of a priggish school-girl, captain of the hockey team, a prefect and a recent candidate for confirmation.'

His lordship was left in no doubt about the risk of making such comments. He was threatened with shooting and whipping, and words took practical effect when after a television interview, he was heartily slapped in the face by an irate onlooker.

♪ 6 Stability and Change

Talking to Lord Boyd Orr in Cairo in 1951 the corpulent King Farouk of Egypt remarked with almost prophetic accuracy: 'There will soon be only five kings left – the Kings of England, Diamonds, Spades, Hearts and Clubs'. Maybe Farouk had had with uncanny insight a vision of his own destiny. In any event there was already ample precedent to give substance to his words; Europe was strewn with the wreckage of royal dynasties.

Warnings had sounded with clarion clearness at the birth of the century. First, in 1906 an anarchist's bomb had burst beneath the carriage of the showy Alfonso XIII of Spain. The death toll had been high but the King survived, a fate not granted to Carlos of Portugal who succumbed to an assassin's bullet two years later. At Sarajevo in 1914 the Archduke Franz Ferdinand, the refined heir apparent to the throne of the Austro-Hungarian Empire, fell to the bomb which crudely detonated the First World War, itself a ruthless destroyer of monarchies. Four years earlier the Braganza throne of Portugal had collapsed under the furious onslaught of revolution. The Hohenzollerns in Germany, the Habsburgs in Austria, the Romanovs in Russia and the Montenegrin throne were cruelly swept away in the deluge of war. In 1937 the Spanish Bourbons collapsed under bludgeoning revolution; the monarchies in Bulgaria, Rumania and Yugoslavia foundered beyond rescue in the cataclysm of the Second World War; and in its aftermath Italy's House of Savoy receded ingloriously before a republic.

Strangely, though most monarchies have crashed, the House of Windsor grows stronger in the hearts of the people. That

Queen Elizabeth reigns but does not rule is a formula which many foreigners regard as mere frivolity. They cannot comprehend why the British pride themselves on being a democracy in which the people choose their rulers – the House of Commons – and yet claim that the sovereign reigns over the land. On the surface this seems illogical, but the British have never created a logical system of government, any more than they have formulated a *written* constitution. They prefer to adapt themselves to prevailing conditions.

To a great extent the British monarchy (after attaining its zenith of power in the years of the Tudors) has reverted to the early origins of kingship, to the primitive times when in many communities the leader was as much priest as king. He was the focal point of tribal ceremonial, the custodian of the rights of the people, God's regent on earth and so everyone obeyed the laws and customs. Whether he made the laws is debatable; in primitive societies law was often custom, based on the traditions of the tribal elders. Moreover the king (or *Cyning*, as he was known in Anglo-Saxon times) did not necessarily enforce the law. Yet an offence committed near him entailed severer punishment because it intruded on his *peace*. The question of maintaining the sovereign's peace would grow into a fundamental factor in English law and life.

There is a parallel in the status of Queen Elizabeth, but in a more sophisticated form. She is secular head of the Church, the laws are formulated and enacted in her name, and anyone who disturbs the Queen's peace is brought before the judiciary which acts on her behalf. This does not imply that Elizabeth II is an indolent queen in the communal hive. Indeed her father George VI rightly compared his royal duties to those of the chairman of an international corporation: in his case the combine comprised Britain and the rest of the Commonwealth. Yet, unlike his counterpart in a world-wide commercial enterprise (or indeed the president of a republic), he could never anticipate retirement, ridding himself of the problems of State. It was compulsory that the sovereign remained on duty every hour of the day for the whole of his life. And in the end the Queen's father died from the strain.

In her role as Queen Elizabeth II is neither an anachronism nor a luxury financed by the taxpayer. Even in Britain, and certainly overseas, some people imagine the sovereign to be nothing more than the central figure in the nation's pomp and pageantry; briefly, a medieval puppet posing as head of Britain's affairs. Nothing could be more inaccurate. Queen Elizabeth is no cipher and the glittering ceremonial of monarchy is merely the outer trappings hiding the true significance in the Queen's role; for it is a paradox of British history that, in the centuries-old process of denuding the monarchy of despotic power, Parliamentary democracy has evolved a sovereign whose days are taxed severely.

Not that the ritual can be discounted or even discarded. Today the people demand it as much as they ever did – a truism which haunted Queen Victoria. As Queen Empress she was one of the world's most powerful figures, yet while she remained in purdah she fanned the embers of republicanism and antagonized her subjects. The British want to see their monarch on parade and it was only when the diminutive, black-clothed figure presented herself to the people amid a panoply of splendour that she regained the people's hearts. Her gregarious son Edward VII to whose pleadings she finally yielded, never made his mother's mistake. His reign teemed with royal pageantry and his reign became synonymous with the grandiose spectacle. Shrewdly he revived the old custom whereby the monarch opened Parliament in person.

Whether due to natural acumen or sane counsel, Queen Elizabeth has never neglected this facet of monarchy. And although television can justifiably be accused of inspiring certain social evils, at least it is the priceless tool of monarchy; it takes the Queen into the people's homes, creating an intimacy which has never been so close.

King George V, the founder of modern social monarchy, had a genuine desire to increase the links with his subjects. But at first he shrank from the new medium of sound broadcasting. As

13 (*Above*) George the Good is dead, and Sir George Bellew, Garter King at Arms, reads the accession proclamation of the late King's daughter, Queen Elizabeth II, at Friary Court, St James's Palace, London.

14 Built in 1762 for George III, the State coach, which is used solely for coronations, was renovated extensively before the Queen's crowning. Using surgeons' scalpels, experts removed the seven famous Cipriani panels, which were scratched, then remounted them.

15 and 16 Tradition persists down the centuries. In the print below, from a fifteenth-century manuscript illustrating the coronation of Henry IV in 1399, the throne is raised on a 'mount' or 'scaffold' approached by four steps. The Queen's throne, which was also raised and approached by four steps, is shown in this photograph above, in which Prince Philip is seen paying homage.

17 The regalia consists of symbols of the monarch's temporal power. Wearing her Coronation Robe and the fabulous Imperial State Crown, the Queen holds the Royal Sceptre and the Orb of England.

18 The history of the regalia is thought to have begun in the reign of Edward the Confessor. His Great Seals reveal him holding items of the regalia – as, for instance, the Sceptre and Orb (illustrated below).

19 (*Above left*) St Edward's Crown contains some 440 precious and semi-precious stones. The velvet Cap of Estate was a badge of rank which at times replaced the royal crown.

20 (*Left*) The Ampulla and the Anointing Spoon are the two most ancient objects used at coronations.

21 (*Opposite above*) *Magna Carta* – the charter of liberties. Illustrated is a portion of a remaining copy of this celebrated document sealed in the reign of King John.

22 (*Opposite below*) Friction between the Roman Catholic James II and his Parliament led to the invitation to the Protestant William of Orange, husband of Mary, James's eldest daughter, to 'bring over an army and secure the infringed liberties' of the country.

23 Among other matters, the Declaration of Rights stressed the endeavour of James and his Ministers 'to subvert and extirpate the Protestant Religion and the Lawes and Libertyes of this Kingdome'. The subsequent Act of Settlement enforced the union between Protestant Church and Protestant monarch.

24 (Below) Attended by her Yeomen of the Guard, the Queen visits Westminster Abbey for the Maundy service. The ceremony related originally to Christ's washing of his disciples' feet. The monarch no longer cleanses the feet of the poor but distributes Maundy Money.

25 (*Above*) Made of silver, Maundy coins consist of penny, half groat or twopenny, threepenny and a groat or fourpenny pieces. The penny was the Norman *sterling* (so christened because it bore a star) from which the British name their currency.

26 Out of the organised party system emerged the office of Prime Minister. From the subsequent sharp fluctuations of political fortunes monarchy had inevitably to disentangle itself. Sir Robert Walpole (whose administration lasted from 1721–42) is hailed as 'the first Prime Minister'.

27 Parliament comprises the sovereign, Lords and Commons. This is graphically illustrated at the State Opening of Parliament when the Queen reads from the throne in the House of Lords the speech outlining the government's programme for the new session.

28 This print showing the first Elizabeth with her Parliament reveals striking continuity of ceremony. As at a modern State Opening, the judges sit on the inner Woolsacks while the Lords, spiritual and temporal, occupy the benches. The Speaker and Commons stand behind the bar at the rear. The main Woolsack, the Lord Chancellor's seat, is vacant because the Queen is present.

29 (Above) To take their seats, members of the Lords and Commons must first receive a writ from the Queen. Illustrated is an early writ of summons to Parliament, dated 1274.

30 (Below) The Speaker of the House of Commons presenting his speech to the Queen at a ceremony held in historic Westminster Hall to commemorate the 700th aniversary of Parliament. It recalled the bitter seventeenth-century struggle between the sovereign and Parliament and the eventual rise of the Cabinet.

31 Westminster Hall, meeting place of the monarch's Great Council, out of which grew the Courts of Justice and Parliament, was the setting of the trial of Charles I which changed the course of English monarchy and added to the power of the Commons.

32 Here Queen Elizabeth makes her first Christmas Day broadcast to listeners all over the world in 1952.

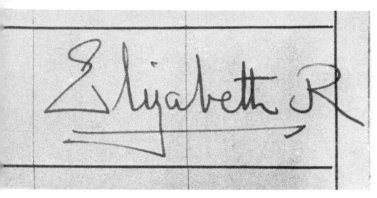

33 (*Above*) A copy of the Queen's signature as it appears on State documents. Parliamentary Bills and Orders in Council – the most important documents – are not signed but receive Her Majesty's assent.

34 (*Below*) Much of the Queen's time is spent at her desk reading correspondence, State papers, despatches from the Cabinet and Departments, and the Commonwealth. She follows debates in Parliament through the *Official Report*. All documents arrive in leather-covered cases called Boxes.

35 (*Left*) Prince Charles, the Heir Apparent, is presented by the Queen to the people of the Principality after his investiture as Prince of Wales in July 1969 in the grounds of ancient Caernarvon Castle. This is the most important title which the Queen can confer.

36 (*Below*) Each June on her official birthday the Queen takes the salute at the traditional Trooping the Colour ceremony – a ritual which began so each man would recognise his flag in battle.

37 In the paddock at Windsor. Like the Queen, Princess Anne has great affection for horses. She has just unsaddled William, the pony on which she and Prince Charles learnt to ride.

38 During June the Queen – the 'fount of honour' – attends the Knights of the Garter ceremony in St George's Chapel, Windsor. The Orders in her personal gifts are the Garter, the Thistle, the Royal Victorian, and the Order of Merit. All other honours are given on the recommendation of British and Commonwealth Prime Ministers.

39 Many organisations, both in Britain and abroad, seek portraits of the Queen. Timothy Whidborne's portrait of Her Majesty was commissioned by the Irish Guards.

the Duke of Windsor revealed in his book, *Crown and People* :

> The fact is not generally known that it was Queen Mary who
> finally persuaded my father to make his annual Christmas
> broadcast to the British Empire. A number of others, includ-
> ing myself, had tried in vain to induce him to use the
> wonderful new medium of the radio. But he would have
> none of it, associating the 'wireless' with electioneering and
> the British equivalent of soap opera. However, my mother
> saw the advantage to the monarchy of the King's being able
> to reach in this way millions of his subjects whom he had
> never seen and who would otherwise never even hear his
> voice. He gave in to her with misgivings and without enthu-
> siasm. But, delighted with the world-wide acclaim of the first
> experiment, he came to take a secret pride in the preparation
> and delivery of each Christmas message.

Both George vi and Elizabeth ii continued this innovation
which roused phenomenal world interest. Conclusive proof
came in 1969. Because television viewers had seen the Queen at
the investiture of the Prince of Wales at Caernarvon and at
Christmas service in St George's, Windsor, as well as in the
royal film, she decided against broadcasting at Christmas that
year. The gust of widespread disappointment in Britain and the
Commonwealth, the United States and many other countries
caused her to resume the broadcast for Christmas 1970.

Continuing the work begun by her grandfather Elizabeth ii
has brought the throne nearer to the people by introducing
new or modifying old institutions and customs. Thus she has
destroyed the myth that she is the centre of a governing clique.
She abandoned, for instance, the presentation parties at which
the daughters of the leaders of the social hierarchy made their
obeisance before the monarch on emerging into adult life.
Years ago sour-tongued cynics described these events as parades
of eligible brides for the princes of the royal family – a fallacy
considering that by custom they seemed to marry German
princesses. And each year she entertains thousands of people of
every rank during the summer at Buckingham Palace and

Holyroodhouse. There has also been a broadening of awards in the Birthday and New Year Honours Lists.

The puzzling thing about the Queen's popularity is that it does not rest on political strength. In fact the power of the Crown dwindled under her great-great-grandmother, but the prestige of the British monarchy blossomed from that period. Queen Victoria did not merely personify her times but was the embodiment of a great empire. In her fretful moments she defied the politicians – on occasions impetuously hinting at abdication – but she had the wit to appreciate that the monarchy's survival rested upon its divorce from politics. Intelligently in the main she hoisted it beyond the rancour of political controversy and thereby gave it strength. Apart from this the new status of monarchy was forced on Queen Victoria due to the transmutation of the British social and political scene. Out of the Industrial Revolution came the series of Reform Acts which swelled the franchise and out of the conflict of political doctrines emerged the organized party system we know today, each faction struggling for the support of a public whose opinion was becoming more enlightened. It led to the creation of the office of Prime Minister and the rise and fall of party fortunes. Party leaders could obviously succeed each other after regaining popular favour, but for a sovereign to get entangled in party battles – leading one and then the other – would have placed the monarch in an impossible dilemma. The royal family had no alternative but to retreat for good from the political arena.

At first Queen Victoria disliked the party system feeling, as a constitutional monarch, 'guilty of dishonesty in giving her confidence suddenly to persons who had been acting in opposition to those to whom she had hitherto given it'. Such things embarrassed her and she would have preferred a coalition. Later this attitude changed due to her dislike of Gladstone: 'for I never could have the slightest particle of confidence in him after his violent, mischievous and dangerous conduct for the last three years'.

The intellectual Prince Albert, who was better informed than many Cabinet Ministers (it was claimed that in Britain's dealing with foreign countries he 'got the government out of innumerable scrapes'), was shaping monarchy into what has been described as 'an indispensable occasional department of State' when he died.

However, the prerogatives of the sovereign in Victoria's reign were the dissolution and convocation of Parliament, the election and dismissal of Ministers, mercy, the creation of peers, the nomination of official appointments and the declaration of war and peace, the making of treaties and the cession of territory. Although Queen Anne in 1701 had been the last monarch to exercise that right (and the last of the British monarchy to preside at Cabinet meetings), Queen Victoria was still empowered to refuse her assent to a Parliamentary Bill, even in defiance of the Lords and Commons.

Elizabeth II also enjoys that privilege, but only in theory. As Walter Bagehot, a constitutional authority in Victorian times, observed, the British monarch 'could disband the army; she could dismiss all the officers . . . she could sell off all our ships-of-war and all our naval stores . . . she could make every citizen in the United Kingdom, male or female, a peer; she could make every parish in the United Kingdom a "University"; she could dismiss most of the civil servants, and she could pardon all offenders'.

By interpreting the law of the land in its strictest sense, Queen Elizabeth is endowed with all these rights, although she would never attempt to fulfil such an eccentric programme. Indeed in practice she lacks the power to enforce it. Her task is to personify authority and not to dictate in British and Commonwealth affairs. As Head of State the Queen acts on the advice of Ministers, and she can only impose her will by means of documents which indicate the approval of the Privy Council or any of her Ministers.

Even so she is the heart of the constitution, the source of all legal energy and the only lawful origin of constitutional authority. The judges adminster justice in her name and the members of the Cabinet are technically her servants and

advisers. Moreover, Parliament cannot sit to debate its programme without her proclamation. Neither can the Members
of either House take their seats without first receiving her writ.
Thus each Parliament is summoned, prorogued or dissolved by
a personal visit of the Queen or by a Commission representing
her under her Great Seal.

Yet it is one of those political oddities that although the
Palace of Westminster is royal property the Queen is debarred
from entering the House of Commons. This act of independence by the people's Chamber reflects an historically significant incident in 1642. It was the day Charles I entered the
Lower Chamber with his troops to arrest five Members whom
he accused of treason. So great had the power of the Commons
become that Speaker Lenthall refused to disclose where they
had fled, making that classic remark: 'May it please Your
Majesty, I have neither eyes to see, nor tongue to speak in this
place, but as this House is pleased to direct me'. The King left
the Chamber in a huff and no successor has entered it officially
ever since. Even the Queen's troops must stay outside the
boundary of the Palace of Westminster unless the Speaker
permits them to cross it.

The Queen, however, is an integral part of the political
machine. Actually Parliament consists of the monarch and the
Lords and Commons. All three form the legislature, but on only
one day each year, in late October or early in November, do
they assemble under one roof. This is for the State Opening of
Parliament. The ceremony begins with the blare of trumpets
and the clatter of horses' hoofs as the Queen, accompanied by
Prince Philip, sets off from Buckingham Palace in the Irish state
coach. The rumbling wheels and tinkling cavalry in scarlet and
blue and the gleaming helmets on tossing heads never fail to
attract the cheering crowds who are witnessing a thousand
years of the nation's history. For Parliament was an offshoot of
the monarchy, first the Lords and then the Commons.

Long before the Queen has entered Westminster, her
Yeomen of the Guard (founded in 1485 at the coronation of
Henry VII) have already searched the basement rooms of the

Houses of Parliament – an annual rite dating from a November day in 1605 when Guy Fawkes and other Catholic conspirators tried to blow up James 1 and his Parliament. Sticklers for tradition the Yeomen, the most ancient royal bodyguard and the world's oldest military corps, incongruously carry lamps although the cellars are illuminated with electricity. With them nowadays are members of the Special Branch of the Metropolitan Police Force who protect the Queen and her family.

Although it is morning the Queen is wearing evening dress and in the grandeur of the Robing Room near the House of Lords she dons her crimson, ermine-lined robe of state, replaces her diadem (composed of Maltese cross and national emblems) with the Imperial State Crown, then proceeds to the Lords' Chamber, taking her place on Pugin's magnificent throne, the primary throne in her kingdom. It is a scene which reverberates down the corridors of time: the monarch meeting in the Parliament House to parley with her Lords Spiritual and Temporal.

But as yet Parliament is not complete: Elizabeth 11 awaits 'the faithful Commons'. At her signal Black Rod, her officer in the House of Lords, summons the people's representatives, the Members of Parliament. Traditionally the door of the Commons is slammed in Black Rod's face and opened only after his third knock – a blunt reminder of the Chamber's independence. Then, proceeding to the Lords, both Government and Opposition Members pair off, led by the Prime Minister and the leader of the Opposition.

The main purpose of this pageantry, known as the 'Queen in Parliament', is to hear the speech which, prepared by her Ministers, outlines the Government's programme for that parliamentary session.

Taking the speech from the Purse (a memento of the time when the holder of this office was the sovereign's Chief Minister), the Lord Chancellor hands it to the Queen. She expounds her Government's policies and sets the stage for yet another year of parliamentary debates. Bills will be passed in both Houses but none will be written into the law of the land as an Act of Parliament until Queen Elizabeth has given her royal assent in ancient Norman-French : *'La reyne le veult'*.

In legal theory, therefore, the Queen enacts the nation's laws and is the only lawful origin of constitutional authority; indeed during the weeks when governments are changed all power is vested in the monarch. In practice the interregnum is merely a matter of hours; for the outgoing Ministers stay in office until they are actually succeeded, on condition that they postpone any controversial decisions. When they hand back their seals of office to the Queen she immediately summons the new Ministers to receive them.

Within this theoretical framework Elizabeth II is the author of executive acts; issuing orders, making appointments to office, conducting international affairs, and commanding all the armed forces. But although she lends both her name and signature the decisions made in her name and the documents which she signs emanate from the Ministers themselves. It is singular that the two most important class of document – Acts of Parliament and Orders in Council – receive the Queen's assent *verbally*.

Cynics might say that, in the circumstances, British monarchy is obsolete; that Queen Elizabeth is little more than a cipher. The fact is that no Parliament has as yet denied the sovereign the power to refuse her assent. The Queen, therefore, still retains the power to veto a Bill. In the normal course of events this prerogative would never be applied. Even Queen Victoria, who interfered in the affairs of government in a manner which would be intolerable today and who sometimes threatened to refuse her assent, finally always yielded. But the Queen guarantees an obstacle in extreme necessity should anyone try to foist on to the nation anything which was unconstitutional. She is therefore the nation's guardian of the constitution.

She cannot stop politicians from making buffoons of themselves or uttering specious promises at election time. She cannot guarantee that Ministers will not plunge into acts of folly or even abuse their powers, but she can ensure that no one but Parliament can make laws in her name. Indeed, it would be a breach of her coronation oath if she entrusted the seals of office to any Ministers who lacked the support of Parliament. Also the courts would decline to accept the authority of decrees issued by parvenu Ministers. Consequently while the monarchy survives there can be no *Reichstag*, for it would never receive the sovereign's proclamation.

Bagehot contended that Queen Victoria 'must sign her own death warrant if the two Houses unanimously send it up to her'. If that is true then it also applies to her great-great-granddaughter. However, more recent constitutional authorities have challenged this bald assertion. On the eve of the First World War during the controversy on Irish Home Rule Sir William Anson backed the Conservative claim that King George v possessed powers as 'guardian of the constitution'. Sir Ivor Jennings also stood firm on the contention that the sovereign had the right of veto to a policy 'which subverted the democratic basis of the constitution.'

No matter how the constitutionalists argue the monarchy is undoubtedly a weighty stabilizing factor in national affairs, and more so in times of crisis. The degree of stability, of course, is influenced by the experience and personality of the sovereign. The Queen's grandfather was rather uncertain of himself early in his reign. Indeed Bonar Law is on record as having bragged: 'I think I have given the King the worst five minutes that he has had for a long time.' To what extent this humiliation is true is uncertain. Yet few would question George v's wisdom in statecraft years later.

In 1931, during the calamitous days of the economic debacle, George v was no longer a fledgling monarch. He had accumulated twenty-one years of kingship and all timidity had gone. Without doubt he was the architect of the National Government and by this shrewd manoeuvre he rescued Britain from disaster. Fortunately Britain was not a republic. The impartial King, aloof from political bias and intrigue, could act swiftly, confident that the whole of the nation trusted him, a confidence which might easily have been denied to a partisan president.

During the revolutionary aftermath of the Second World War, when Britain was racked by disorder and disunity and amid the uncertainties came the strident voices of political conflict, at the heart of everything stood the sobering figure of the King, the hereditary, living representative of Britain's history down the ages and vital proof of the continuity of the British way of life.

In this permissive age when morality seems so often at a discount, and politicians themselves are sometimes prone to add to the rot, the Queen's dignity and high standards, combined with her charm and friendliness, are prominent on the national scene. Summing up the situation in homespun words, an American professor remarked: 'On our side of the Atlantic we have a great respect for your Queen. She seems to be the only person in this goddam country who is trying to keep up any standards.'

The weight given to the Queen's words and actions is indirectly the product down the years of the people themselves. By evolving their system of constitutional monarchy, the British have produced a wholly *national representative*. When Queen Elizabeth speaks or acts she does so for the nation as a whole. It is in that sense that the British accept laws and orders in the Queen's name. Therefore, as someone once stressed, when Queen Elizabeth sits on the throne, it is in effect the enthronement of the common man.

A shrewd sovereign who has spent many years on the throne can be the country's greatest repository of knowledge of state affairs. As Bagehot pointed out, the sovereign has the right to be consulted, to encourage and to warn. The Queen is informed and consulted daily. The Prime Minister regularly communicates to her Cabinet deliberations, the course of policy, the conduct of negotiations and the whole range of executive action. Each day when Parliament is sitting she receives a specially written summary of its proceedings.

Queen Victoria wielded appreciable influence over her

Ministers due to her accumulated knowledge of many years. In fact, in the latter stages of her long reign she could comment on events which occurred before some Ministers were even born. There is the classic illustration when Campbell-Bannerman, then Secretary of State for War, sought the Queen's approval to what he believed to be an innovation in the Army. But he was quickly disillusioned. 'No, Mr Bannerman', she replied. 'Lord Palmerston proposed exactly the same thing to me in '52, and Lord Palmerston was wrong.'

The monarch's guidance is perhaps all the more necessary today. Members of Parliament, and therefore Ministers, are drawn from a wide variety of spheres. This is commendable, but not all necessarily possess adequate experience of public life. Moreover Ministers, even Prime Ministers, come and go, whereas the monarch holds office for life. Thus it is vital that the Head of State should be sufficiently knowledgeable to cite precedents and submit arguments in support of a point.

What is equally valuable is that the monarch thinks in national terms and not within narrow partisan confines. This was revealed by Clement Attlee, one of four Prime Ministers during the fifteen-year reign of George VI. At the time of the King's death he commented, 'It is one of the privileges of a Prime Minister to be able to discuss affairs of State with a man who is above the political battle, and who has had a long and continuous experience both of things and persons. I knew, too, that I would always get from him a well-balanced judgement.' Winston Churchill said, 'I made certain he was kept informed of every secret matter, and the care and thoroughness with which he mastered the immense daily flow of State papers made a deep mark on my mind.'

Speaking of Queen Elizabeth in a television interview Sir Alec Douglas-Home, a former Prime Minister, once said that he felt quite certain that he was speaking for every British Prime Minister when he described the weekly meeting with the Queen as of 'great value'. 'The Queen has a very wide experience', he went on, 'and happily an ever-widening experience. . . . She knows every Commonwealth Prime

Minister from her tours in the Commonwealth and from Commonwealth meetings in London, and I should think every Commonwealth statesman personally.... The Queen has the continuing advice of Prime Ministers and Ministers over the years. And this is valuable because Governments can change, sometimes can change very often. The Queen is therefore able to put a continuing point of view.'

The Queen had chosen Sir Alec as Prime Minister, for it is still the monarch's function to decide on the premiership. Indeed the initial step in forming a new government is taken by the sovereign. In most cases the choice is automatic; nowadays it is customary to appoint the elected leader of the political party which commands a majority in the House of Commons. But when there is no clearly designated leader the onus of choice rests with the sovereign. When, for instance, failing health compelled Bonar Law, the Conservative Prime Minister, to resign in 1923, he declined to advise the sovereign on a suitable successor. It was generally believed that Lord Curzon, who was the dominant and senior member of the Conservative Party, would be elected. Yet to widespread astonishment, George v, after discussions with others (although he could have ignored their counsel), invited Stanley Baldwin, Chancellor of the Exchequer, to accept the appointment.

This situation is much more complicated when the electorate give no party a working majority. Such intricacies arose in 1924. When the Baldwin Government fell George v had the choice of summoning Asquith, the Liberal leader, Ramsay MacDonald, who led the Socialists, or a politician sufficiently powerful to form a coalition. Finally he sent for MacDonald whose backing was no more than about one-third of the Commons.

Churchill was favoured at the expense of Halifax, and in the Queen's own reign she had the uneviable task when Harold Macmillan resigned. As the retiring Prime Minister Macmillan lacked the constitutional right to advise the Queen yet she asked for his guidance. Macmillan named Sir Alec Douglas-Home in preference to two other contenders. Queen Elizabeth was under no compulsion to accept his suggestion and it has been said that in so doing she created a precedent. Rightly or wrongly her action was the reverse of her great-great-grandmother's in 1852. When Lord Derby resigned the premiership he advised Queen Victoria to nominate Lord Lansdowne as his successor. But Prince Albert, an astute student of the constitution, rightly pointed out that, since he was no longer a Minister, he could not tender advice. Thus Queen Victoria sent for Lord Aberdeen and not Lord Lansdowne.

The right to dissolve Parliament is not entirely the Prime Minister's prerogative. If Queen Elizabeth in her role as guardian of the people's liberties, had proof that this power was being abused, she could obstruct the dissolution. In this respect the Queen's right stems from the basic principle that the sovereign must always remain impartial. For this reason the royal prerogative must never be applied for political gain.

A remarkable example of the Crown's impartiality was illustrated in 1913 by King George V, in whose reign, incidentally, the modern conception of British constitutional monarchy was stabilized. Union politicians and the opponents of Irish Home Rule demanded that he should dissolve Parliament without 'advice' from the Liberal Government. This political manoeuvre was ridiculous, for the monarchy would never in normal circumstances dissolve Parliament without the agreement of the respective Ministers. If the King had heeded the Unionists' false claim that their political rivals had no 'mandate' for Irish Home Rule the monarchy would have ceased to be impartial, having allied itself with the Unionist movement.

One should point out, however, that in a legal sense the Queen could dissolve Parliament – in the way, for instance, that Charles II did in 1680 – without consulting the Ministers. But it would be a hazardous thing to do, for it would be tantamount to dismissing them and appealing to the country in a general election to support a new government which would take retrospective responsibility for the monarch's action in dismissing their predecessors. It would therefore be staking the survival of the Crown on the result of the election and could only be contemplated as a last resort in a revolutionary situation. This in itself indicates that the sovereign does not automatically agree to any suggestion submitted by the politicians. Normally, for example, the monarch would confer a peerage on anyone recommended by the Prime Minister, assuming that the character of the person involved was beyond reproach. Yet the sovereign would doubtless refuse to collaborate in creating peers so that one party might have an overwhelming majority in the Lords for a specific political manoeuvre.

However, King George v pledged himself to create peers, if necessary, to pass the Parliament Bill in 1911. True, it was imperative that the Liberal Government should get a renewed mandate from the electorate, yet the promise to create the peers was not lightly made. The Parliament Bill was the successful attempt by the Commons to deprive the Lords of all power to reject a money Bill, and to reduce their power to delay other Bills. This Liberal action roused hostility from the Lords who had the alliance of the Tories in the Commons. The King had many intimate friends among the Tories, a party to which he was closer than any other faction, yet he refused to let them use his name to defeat the will of the people.

By co-operating in the passage of the Reform Bill of 1832, thus giving the vote to many more people and making the House of Commons more democratic, and in the passage of the Parliament Act of 1911, which made the House of Lords less able to thwart the decisions of the Lower Chamber, the monarchy demonstrated its willingness to ensure the rights of the people. It was not that the respective monarchs became, either in 1832 or 1911, political partisans, who championed one of the opposing sides. That would not have been the legal way to effect change. They did a far better thing – something which echoes in the relationship between monarchy and people today. They acted in obedience to the unwritten rule of national life which prescribes that the powers of the monarch shall be used in accordance with the will of the nation. They were beyond party strife, their interests were devoted to the nation as a whole, and they joined with the people generally in bringing about change when the will of the nation was set for change.

That is really why the British monarchy has survived; it is also the reason why Queen Elizabeth sits on the throne today. She reigns because for the past three centuries British sovereigns have abandoned earlier pretensions, learnt new lessons and altered their role to cope with changing times.

In the eighteenth century, for instance, they adopted a new status due to the development of a Cabinet system and the growth of the office of Prime Minister. One cannot ignore the fact that the early Hanoverians accepted that growth largely because the first Georges, preferring Hanover to England, neglected their governmental duties and transferred them to Ministers. The ambitious George III strenuously tried to regain the authority that his two predecessors had abandoned to the Chief Minister. He made progress for a while through the 'King's friends', a monarchist element, and through bribery. Certainly he undermined the power of the Whigs, but the politicians finally became alive to his motives and his periods of illness also worked against him. Whether he suffered from bouts of insanity or whether his eccentricities were the outcome of porphyria (a poisoning of the nervous system which affects the brain), by 1811 he was so sick that his reprobate son – the future George IV – was appointed Prince Regent. There is little doubt that the Hanoverians loosened the thread of monarchical power. By the time of Queen Victoria's accession she could embarrass her Ministers by her independence, but she would not wield real power. Gradually the monarch's personal intervention in the machinery of government grew less. Today Queen Elizabeth is seen in a niche which her great-great-grandmother carved out for limited monarchy. Even before he abdicated her uncle Edward VIII had demonstrated that he could not on the grounds of temperament accept the limitations imposed on monarchy. The Queen's father restored confidence in the monarchy and today it is still, in the main, as it was in Victoria's time – a symbol of unity and a model of what family life should be.

Resisting change itself, European royalty predicted inevitable doom for the British monarchy as it trimmed its sails to the wind of social and political change. Yet history has shown that the prophets themselves have foundered, whereas the British monarchy, in the person of the Queen, has become increasingly secure. That security is partly attributable to the fact that she provides a balancing mechanism, for in Britain equilibrium is achieved in the name of the Crown. In politics, for instance, balance is provided by Her Majesty's Opposition, the counterweight to the Government.

But perhaps more important is the realization that she is a unit of balance in herself. She embodies a fund of *national* political sentiment. She stands apart from the party rancour which separates her Government and her Opposition. It is an active and practical function which is hard to define; for although she acts on the advice of her Ministers she is something separate from them; she represents fears and sentiments in the national life which only she as the hereditary monarch can represent. Not only is she the symbol of unity, but also a magnet of loyalty which attracts men's feelings into the service of the community. Most important of all, it has been rightly claimed that – stable itself and still changing – the monarchy has helped the whole of British national life to combine stability with change.

The progress goes on today. Britain adapted her existing institutions more easily to the changing requirements of the times because she has the flag of monarchy at her masthead and the ballast of monarchy in her hold. The flag may change its quarters as the ship moves on its long voyage; but it always remains the same flag. The ballast may be shifted, this way or that, to suit the state of the currents and the roll of the ship. But the balance is always there.

§ 7 The Magical Power

In 1847, the year of Queen Victoria's Golden Jubilee, the idea that the British Empire was destructible – either by physical or peaceful means – would have seemed a wild conjecture. The small, dumpy figure – repeated in stone in many lands – gazed with stern benignity on the greatest Empire the world has known. It was the proud boast that the sun never set on Victoria's realms; that millions of subjects of varied colour and creed shared the protection of the Great White Queen. It was the culmination of five centuries of colonial growth, beginning when John Cabot, sent by Henry VII to discover new lands, came across Newfoundland. More than two centuries ago Britain had founded her first Empire, and virtually controlled the whole of North America. And although the thirteen American colonies were lost roughly a century later the British exercised power over an even greater Empire: a quarter of the globe.

Yet although Victoria's Empire seemed durable for ever, some sixty years after her Golden Jubilee the Union Jack was lowered for the last time over the viceregal palace in New Delhi. India had been the glittering jewel of the second Empire, a source of English wealth and power since the last day of the year 1600 when the first Elizabeth granted a charter to the East India Company. The object then had not been territory but the trade in cinnamon and pepper, nutmeg and cloves so eagerly sought in Europe. But gradually by trade and conquest (due partly to the ambitions of France), British rule over the sub-continent was made secure.

Over the years the Crown's influence on India was indirect,

even though the Company acted under the direction of the British Government. Indeed it was not until 1857, after the disastrous Indian Mutiny, that the control of almost one-fifth of the human race passed into official influence. The Act of 1858 for the Better Government of India dissolved the Company and gave direct control to the Crown.

But there were British statesmen who, years earlier, had predicted that Indians would wish to rule themselves. In the Commons in 1833 Lord Macaulay declared, 'Having become instructed in European knowledge, they may, in some future age, demand European institutions ... whenever it comes it will be the proudest day in English history'.

But the struggle for independence was long and difficult and it was not until 15 August 1947 that nationalist demands were finally met. India and Pakistan emerged from what was British India. Many hailed independence as a sign of British weakness; in actual fact it was partly the result of a natural course of events, partly due to British exhaustion in the turmoil of war. From that time the Empire started to shrink. Other British possessions demanded autonomy and received it, and from the British Empire was born the Commonwealth of Nations.

That is the main dissimiliarity between the monarchy of Queen Victoria and that of Queen Elizabeth. The former was the Queen Empress of an immense Empire; the latter the Head of the Commonwealth. Signs of what have been described as the abandonment of Empire grew more distinct while the Queen was Princess Elizabeth. On 21 April 1947, her twenty-first birthday, making her dedication broadcast in Cape Town she announced to Britain and the Empire : 'I declare before you all that my whole life, whether it be long or short, shall be devoted to your service and the service of our great Imperial Family to which we all belong. . . .' Even then the day was fast approaching when South Africa and India would withdraw from the imperial family, and before 1947 had ended the masses of India were contending that the time had arrived for self-government.

It has been recorded that King George vi forcefully made it

known to the Labour Government of the time that he was not wholehearted in the granting of independence to British India, claiming that 'India must be governed', and that to release Gandhi from gaol would be absurd. A body of Conservatives fulminated that the King Emperor had been compelled by the Attlee administration to divest himself of his imperial role. Against this, however, there is also the claim that the King not only approved but actually persuaded his second cousin Lord Louis Mountbatten to become the twenty-ninth (and, as events proved, the last) Viceroy of India.

Mountbatten, unravelling the sub-continent's tangled political and social skein, made it clear to both King and Government that the only real solution was the setting up of two independent States. Hence India, shedding the imperial past completely, chose to be a republic, and Pakistan elected at first to be a dominion. India, however, while discarding the sovereign as its supreme head, still desired to participate in the Commonwealth – a curious situation. The formula which was accepted at the Commonwealth Conference in London in April 1949 and which met Indian aspirations was partly inspired by the King himself. When the session concluded Dominion and Indian Prime Ministers expressed their thanks at Buckingham Palace. Profoundly affected King George vi humbly replied, 'Do not thank me. It is to Almighty God, who, I am sure, has led you, that all your thanks should now be given.'

That is why his daughter Elizabeth ii is today Head of a Commonwealth which is a free association of independent States some of which accept her as Queen and republics who do not. At her accession she was proclaimed by varying titles. India did not proclaim her at all, for the head of the India people was now a President not subordinate to the Queen.

Begun in her father's reign, the 'throwing away of the Empire' (as Tory diehards angrily termed it) gathered momentum during the first two decades of Queen Elizabeth's reign. To try to obstruct its advance was futile; one had to accept it, like the onrush of an avalanche. Colonies of Queen Victoria's Empire in Asia, Africa and elsewhere ceased to be governed in the name of Queen Elizabeth II, electing Presidents in her stead. Like South Africa Pakistan has left the Commonwealth completely, and many of the ones who have remained do not even mention the Head of the Commonwealth in their constitutions. And although here and there tatters of British culture linger, each emergent nation is in fact developing its own culture.

Outwardly the Commonwealth presents itself as a loosely defined affiliation of governments with the Crown as a powerless figurehead. Certainly the Queen's nominal role extends to fewer countries than in her father's reign and with it legal authority has diminished. Yet it is debatable if any of her predecessors were received with greater acclamation in countries which formed the old Empire. Compare her visit to India in January 1961 – exactly half a century after her grandfather George V. The King was the first English sovereign to travel to the East since the Crusader Richard Coeur de Lion. He journeyed there in 1911 for his Royal Durbar full of royal ardour to cement closer relations between himself the Emperor of India and his Asian subjects.

'It was entirely my own idea to hold a Coronation Durbar at Delhi in person', he entered in his diary, 'and at first I met with much opposition'. Regrettably the Indians had become attuned to that unfortunate personification of British aloofness and arrogance, Lord Curzon, the Viceroy who had ridden among the people, as an austere and resplendent figure, on an elephant. But now, as a gesture, the King rode among the people on horseback. As King Emperor he had been warmly acclaimed, yet it is doubtful if the cordiality ever reached such dimensions as when, fifty years later after cataclysmic changes in Asia during which India and Pakistan had become republics, his granddaughter (not now Empress of India or even Queen, but merely the symbolic Head of the Commonwealth) set foot on the subcontinent.

How is it that modern British monarchy, stripped of most of its ancient powers, can rouse such ecstatic scenes which no politician could ever hope to stimulate? Perhaps the answer was given in a London *Observer* editorial:

It is worth nothing that the particular British form of monarchy which has shown such exceptional powers, first of survival and then of renaissance, is one which was, in the last century, regarded as particularly weak and 'unreal' by the continental Kings and Emperors of the day: a strictly constitutional form of monarchy, wholly divorced from the political business of government. It is now plain that this divorce, far from weakening the Monarchy, has given it an unsuspected, immeasurable strength. The separation of the Monarchy from the field of 'affairs', of political business, intellectual argument, and rival ambitions has cleared its channels to the subconscious and emotive strata of the collective soul where, we may suspect, lie the deep secret springs of national purpose, character and living unity.... It may well be that the millenium of European Monarchy, when its chief function was the business of ruling, was really a long interlude, and that we have here in Britain, by accident rather than design, stumbled back to the original, true, and abiding function of the Monarchy, which lay in the magical power of Kings – in modern language, in their power to represent, express, and affect the aspirations of the collective sub-conscious. . . .

It may well be that without an organ to fulfil this function, a community and its State is like a body starved of some vitamin, and that this helps to explain the instability of so many recent Republics and their unpredictable propensity to sudden mass-mania, hero-worship and relapse into crude dictatorship. The existence of a constitutional Monarchy, by satisfying profound emotional needs, leaves the business of government to proceed in a quieter, more sober and more rational atmosphere. . . . In the collective soul of the people there is also a deep craving for a figure who represents an ideal; an archetypal figure who, in a phrase originally legal but with a much wider significance, must not be criticized because he 'can do no wrong'.

Science has helped to project the image of modern social monarchy. Jet aircraft, providing a mobility never known to her ancestors, have enabled Elizabeth II to set foot in every country of the Commonwealth. Indeed, she was the first monarch in all history to circumnavigate the globe – a vivid contrast to the first Elizabeth who never went beyond her shores, not even crossing the border into Scotland. The televising of royal events has, moreover, given many people both in Britain and elsewhere a feeling of participation in Queen Elizabeth's life. Television has perhaps done more than any other modern invention to strengthen the ties between Crown and people.

In those Commonwealth countries which owe allegiance to the Queen her formal position is the same as it is in Britain. These countries are not in any way subject to Britain or to one another or to any government representing them all; but each is subject to Queen Elizabeth. For this reason the Queen can have no single Prime Minister, for each self-governing State must obviously have its own Prime Minister and the Queen is separately advised by the individual Prime Ministers of those countries of which she is Queen.

During her father's reign it was hinted that unless the monarch spent long periods with the older members of the Commonwealth the relationship would steadily deteriorate. The proposal collapsed because the sovereign must operate from one central place; for all concerned the ideal focal point is London. But should the question arise once more the Queen now has an adult heir whose royal apprenticeship could mature by periods of residence in the countries concerned. Apart from anything else one would have thought that that would have been an excellent apprenticeship for Prince Charles. Moreover, it would improve the bonds between Britain and other Commonwealth monarchies that have become somewhat frayed since the United Kingdom entered the European Common Market.

The reason why Commonwealth monarchist countries still retain the Queen as their Head of State was pinpointed in a remark by Prime Minister Trudeau during the Commonwealth Conference in Canada in 1973. He observed: 'Why change a system when it works successfully?'

Even if a theorist might suggest the possibility of substituting an elected President for the Queen in Britain the wildest of theorists could scarcely suggest making their hypothetical President the general President and head of all the societies which have issued from the British monarchy. Only one whose ancestors were kings when the first British settlers, traders, navigators and explorers went forth to lay the first foundations – only she can be a symbol and as such the head of the general association which has been built on those foundations.

8 A Family – Not a Dynasty

Napoleon, at the pinnacle of power, was recorded as saying that to be a member of royalty was like playing a theatrical role – but with one exception: the monarch was always at the centre of the stage. Probably to her private dismay at times, Queen Elizabeth occupies the world stage. Her words and actions are seized upon by the British and international press. And with an attitude almost bordering on hysteria, American and continental editors pay fantastic sums for photographs portraying the Queen in poses which would rouse no interest if she were anyone else. This publicity and the ceremonial trappings which surround her give a false impression of her daily routine.

Like the chief executive of any international company she spends many hours at a desk. In spite of her natural shyness there is resilience and toughness beneath the charming exterior – qualities which would have fitted her for a high executive capacity in commerce.

This daily round is no sinecure. Edward VIII openly confessed that he found it irksome. At breakfast the Queen and Prince Philip discuss each other's programme for the day then she proceeds to her study on the first floor of the north wing of Buckingham Palace. There are always flowers on her desk among the photographs of her family and other paraphernalia, including the hour-glass which inaccurately implies that work goes on at a leisurely tempo. A silver tray holds pens and pencils.

As a prelude she reads the London newspapers to familiarize herself with the latest news and current opinion. By tradition her copy of *The Times* is printed on special paper. The Queen has always tended to be an avid reader, partly to broaden her knowledge of life generally. Even though she is unrestricted in her intercourse with the people she relies to a great extent on newspapers, periodicals, television and radio to acquaint herself with the world of ordinary people. Apart from this, it is one of the chores of modern monarchy to possess wide knowledge, if only to maintain an intelligent conversation with the kaleidoscope of people who meet the Queen in any single year. Enthused Dr Konrad Adenauer, when German Chancellor: 'Not only is she charming but she is equally intelligent.'

Usually the Queen's first meeting of the day is with her private secretary to discuss matters demanding prompt attention. Next, with the aid of two assistant private secretaries, she attends to the mail. A spate of letters arrives regularly at the Palace Post Office. When it has been sorted out by her page into the letters written in English and the correspondence from other parts of the world she reads much of the mail herself. It is then dealt with by the private secretaries. All her subjects are entitled to write to her and many never hesitate to do so. Letters vary from appeals for help from the families of people who have fallen foul of the law down to the mentally unstable who misguidedly believe that a letter to the Queen will solve all ills. There are also the usual requests from various bodies for the Queen's presence and she accepts about one in fifty. Letters in unfamiliar languages go to the Foreign Office and, when appropriate, a letter is sent to the Minister responsible, often with a request to be informed of the outcome. People in distress usually have their letters forwarded to a suitable society for investigation and, if necessary, help.

The queen never signs letters (except to close friends) because of the quantity of mail and to thwart autograph hunters from making capital out of her signature. Usually letters (and telegrams) are sent free and are signed by the appropriate household officer. The Palace Post Office is staffed by the Post Office and personnel journey to all the Queen's homes when she moves. No matter where she travels her mail follows her in well-secured leather cases enclosed in chained and padlocked metal boxes. Teleprinters in the telephone room help to cope with the numbers, sometimes amounting to several thousands, of telegrams and cables.

To her mahogany desk go the many despatch boxes, lettered in gold and leather covered, usually in red, containing secret and official documents for her scrutiny and perhaps signature. 'Did my boxes' is the traditional entry in the diary of most British monarchs. At Buckingham Palace only the Queen and her private secretary possess the keys to unlock them. The quantity of official papers at any time depends on whether Parliament is in session or not, and on whether a crisis arises. But irrespective of the volume the work always follows the Queen even when she is touring abroad, for at such times Councillors of State fulfil only certain functions in the United Kingdom. All affairs concerning the Commonwealth must be dealt with by the Queen, no matter where she happens to be. Even a Councillor's duties are limited as a precaution (nowadays only in theory) to prevent power being snatched from the monarch in his or her absence.

On the whole official papers fall into three categories: the more vital documents such as the ones empowering Commissioners to give the royal assent in the House of Lords (that is, the Bills which then become Acts of Parliament); the more routine papers which she must sign – for instance, the appointment of Service chiefs; and, finally, the Cabinet minutes and the despatches circulated by the Foreign and Commonwealth Office to keep the Queen informed.

The Official Report familiarizes her with the debates in Parliament and, adhering to the practice established by her father, each week she receives the Prime Minister for discussion of Cabinet and other topics, usually on Thursday evenings.

This does not include the numerous communications from those Commonwealth countries of which she is Queen. Their correspondence never passes through Whitehall but goes direct to the Queen, either straight from the capitals concerned or through the High Commissioners' Offices in London. Oddly enough the republican countries of the Commonwealth supply the Queen assiduously with secret information even though she no longer has any legal connections with them. Again, this illustrates why a reigning monarch after years in office becomes a store of information unmatched by anyone else in Britain.

Although the monarch has ceased to attend meetings of Ministers Queen Elizabeth still presides in another quarter of constitutional government: the Privy Council. Though the balance of power has long since been reversed the Cabinet, measured in years of service to the State, is a mere stripling beside this age-old body. Indeed the Cabinet was an offshoot of the Council, which has the longevity almost of the institution of monarchy itself. It can be traced back to Norman times and its roots were possibly Saxon, for at that time the monarch sought counsel from the Witanagemot – an assembly of the wise – who met periodically to advise the King. Certainly in Norman times it consisted of the sovereign's tenants-in-chief, household officials and Church leaders. One day its spiritual and temporal peers would emerge as the House of Lords.

The King's Private or Privy Council conducted the day-to-day pattern of government. But as the complexities of national life increased other branches facilitated administration of the country's business. Finance, for instance, hived off to become the Treasury, as did that branch which carried out the law (still retaining the name *Courts*). The central Council, however, still held the reins of royal government, fluctuating in power over the years as the fortunes in the conflict between King and Parliament (first the Lords and then also the Commons) waxed and waned.

Henry VII, that frugal monarch and the first of the Tudors, used it not only as a Council, but as an instrument of fear to suppress rebellion. Meeting in a room in the medieval Palace of Westminster it was given the name of the Star Chamber – so christened because of the pattern on the ceiling.

Surprisingly, Cromwell and his Parliamentarians merely deprived the Council of some of its powers (mainly concerning jurisprudence) and it continued to exist. At the Restoration Charles II relied more on an inner group of five of its members called the Cabal (a word composed of the initial letters of their names). Thus the Cabinet – a name coined because it met in the Cabinet, a room in the King's palace – developed as a significant offspring of the Privy Council.

As Parliament grew more dominant the power of the Privy Council declined. Yet today new life has been injected into it. The modern Parliamentary machine, groaning under the mounting weight of legislation, has welcomed an outlet on which to offload some of its minor items. For Parliamentary procedure can be extremely tedious. The gestation period before the birth of an Act can be lengthy. Yet in the Privy Council the administrative process is swift and requires merely the Queen's verbal assent.

An Order in Council also bears the Privy Council's seal. This is not a waxen seal, but a single-handed seal used for making an impression on paper. A new seal is minted for each reign and the Queen's consists of a rose, thistle and shamrock and crown supported by a lion and unicorn, together with the royal style and titles in Latin.

One of the Council's historic duties is at the commencement of a new reign. It forms the major part of the Accession Council, acclaims the new sovereign and arranges for the public proclamation. After her marriage the Queen, as Princess Elizabeth, lived at Clarence House in the grounds of St James's Palace. She herself was acknowledged at ten o'clock on the morning of 8 February 1952 in the entreé room of the palace, which was the 'Cabinet' of Charles II.

The Privy Council's history actually hinges on committees. The main one is the Cabinet itself. Others have matured into government departments, but technically they are still committees of the Privy Council. Its centuries-old practice of engaging experts for specific functions persists in the form of the Medical Research Council and other specialist bodies. Various committees still exist and the judicial committee is the Council's most important body. In certain situations it is the

Supreme Court of Appeal from Commonwealth countries who accept the Queen as the 'fount of justice'. It is also the final Court of Appeal from the Ecclesiastical Courts.

A Privy Council committee might be set up to investigate a current topic, sometimes of a controversial nature. For instance, a committee to consider better security without affecting individual liberty was set up after the spies Burgess and Maclean defected.

The duties of the Privy Council are very varied. For instance, the Queen in Council prorogues, dissolves and summons Parliament. In the event of hostilities war is declared and treaties are concluded by the Queen in Council. Orders in Council are also used for legislation in international affairs. Royal charters are granted to organizations, and Commonwealth territories, after approval by Parliament, receive their independence. Nowadays much Parliamentary business is placed before it.

Her Majesty can convene meetings of the Privy Council wherever she chooses. They have been held in country homes and even in the royal yacht *Britannia*. But usually they take place at Buckingham Palace in the white and gold 1844 Room, so christened because the Emperor Nicholas of Russia occupied it that year.

At meetings everyone stands. In all there are some three hundred Councillors (with the title of 'Right Honourable') but only three are needed for a quorum. usually four are summoned. Around a small circular table on the Queen's right stands the Lord President, and on her left the Privy Councillors; facing them stands the Clerk. As the Lord President reads the various items of business the Queen gives her verbal approval, then the Clerk signs on her behalf

Extreme secrecy is attached to the wording of a Privy Councillor's oath. Furthermore, there is no question but that it is binding. That is why it is traditional for Cabinet Ministers to be sworn in as Councillors before they assume office. Facing Her Majesty the Minister kneels on the floor as she takes his oath. Then rising, he places his right knee on a stool and 'kisses hands'. Actually he kisses the Queen's right hand before he stands to receive his seal of office. Only the Chancellor of the Duchy of Lancaster receives his seal in private audience.

It is also in Council that the Queen appoints each year the Sheriffs of England and Wales. (Again, those of the Duchy of Lancaster are appointed in private.) This is the monarch's last practical link with justice. Centuries ago justice was dispensed by the King's Court. The monarch ruled with the eminent of the realm (now Parliament), awards were made for courage and service (the equivalent of today's investitures) and the sovereign received men of distinction (as in today's audiences). Although the Law Courts, like Parliament, have gained their independence the Queen is the titular head in the administration of the law.

However, when she appoints the Sheriffs she fulfils a duty; the pricking of the Sheriffs' Roll, which has gone unchanged for centuries. The Roll is of vellum on a wooden roller, and tied with green ribbon. Written in copperplate are all the names for office and with the Bodkin (a device with a steel spike and a round handle engrossed with the Privy Council's arms), the Queen pierces the names of the ones chosen. The story has been handed down that the first Elizabeth, receiving the annual Sheriffs' Roll while sewing in her garden, pricked the names with her bodkin because she had no pen. There is credence for this legend because all earlier Rolls were marked with tiny black dots, but from the days of the Tudor Elizabeth the names have been marked by piercing.

The Queen's daily routine falls into two main categories: her many functions as head of society and her specialized functions as Head of State. Both are exacting. Nowadays the demands on the Queen's presence are so extensive that a year's programme is planned in the early part of the preceding winter. By the end of December she is conversant with her overseas engagements for the next twelve months. In the United Kingdom her major engagements are known about eight months ahead. Public appearances in Britain alone have stepped up enormously. Once during a three-months' stint she completed over two hundred engagements.

Many round-table talks are needed, and many draft plans pass to and fro before the Queen embarks on a journey abroad. It may be a Commonwealth tour or a State visit – an old formal courtesy paid to a friendly nation by the new head of a country. Obviously the purpose is to stimulate better relations, perhaps ridding them of frictions caused by political misunderstandings. The Queen pays one state visit only to any country unless there is a new Head of State.

It has been argued that it is in foreign affairs, rather than in domestic, that the sovereign's influence is particularly felt. The Queen is the centre of that form and ceremony which is nowhere more important than in the solemn relations between one State and another. The very nature of her duties causes her to acquire a wide knowledge of foreign affairs. She can thus give wise, informal advice or quiet warning or encouragement.

Edward VII, whose interests centred more on foreign than domestic matters, proved invaluable in breaking down France's traditional enmity towards his country. Elizabeth II can with justification also claim to be her country's best ambassador. But there is one remarkable difference between her own foreign visits and those of her great-grandfather. Edward VII travelled abroad untrammelled (it might be thought) by the presence of a Minister. Queen Elizabeth, however, is always accompanied by a Minister of State, for the Queen's visits are not only acts of policy and valuable service to the comity and amity of States; there is also a concentrated effort to improve the commercial and cultural atmosphere.

It is the same when the Queen receives new ambassadors; with her is the Foreign Secretary or the Permanent Under-Secretary of State for Foreign Affairs. It is an ancient practice among friendly nations to accredit envoys to the heads of those countries. Diplomats in Britain are accredited to Queen Elizabeth, presenting their Letters of Credence to the Court of St James. Because the Queen no longer resides there this smacks of an anachronism. The custom originates from the days when

St James's Palace and not Buckingham Palace was the monarch's official home.

When George III bought Buckingham Palace for his Queen, it clearly showed his attempt to create a distinction between the sovereign's private and public lives. Until then the King had little privacy. For instance a painting by Houckgeest depicts Charles I and his family dining in Whitehall Palace with the public watching from a nearby gallery. By all accounts the King did not mind, believing that it helped him to assert his authority.

Buckingham Palace became accepted as the King's London home; St James's as the centre of Court ceremonial. Here continued the quarters of the Lord Chamberlain and other household officials; here too, continued the Presence Chamber where the King received ambassadors to the Court of St James. It was not uncommon for official functions to be held at St James's even in Queen Victoria's reign. Some have been held even in our own Queen's reign. But nowadays, on their arrival in Britain, ambassadors are received in the 1844 Room at Buckingham Palace.

Sometimes the Queen gives as many as four or five audiences in a single day to people from different spheres of life. Interspersed are the reading of official papers and other activities. The burden of engagements must therefore be shared by other members of the royal family. Maybe that is one reason why the British have come to put their royal family on a lofty plane: to see in it the ideal of family life to which, in a sense, they would like to aspire themselves.

Actually the British monarchy is no longer regarded as a dynasty but as a family. The Queen is the personification of the State and she must be active in all good works; in short the Queen, aided by her family, must participate in national life by making many public appearances. That is one big difference between British royalty and their counterparts in Scandinavia and Holland. During the Second World War in one three-year period visits totalled more than three thousand – an achievement which caused King George VI to remark, 'We are not a family; we are a firm.' Bagehot put it another way : 'A *family* on the throne is an interesting idea also.'

The nation automatically fixes its gimlet eye on whatever the Queen and the royal family do : a national habit which is sometimes welcomed by politicians. Harassed by problems arising perhaps from their own folly or incompetence, they pray for a royal 'event' to divert the public's attention. Hence the sigh of relief that swept Whitehall when at the height of the Lambton scandal the people's minds were suddenly diverted by the announcement of the engagement of Princess Anne. It must have been the same in Victoria's time, for Bagehot wrote : 'The women – one half of the human race at least – care fifty times more for a marriage than a Ministry . . . a princely marriage is a brilliant edition of a universal fact, and, as such, it rivets mankind'.

The British royal family is extremely closely knit. But most of all the Queen is sustained by her husband Prince Philip to whom, shortly after she came to the throne, the Queen granted 'Place, Pre-eminence and Precedence' next to herself.

There is an impressive parallel between the accession of Queen Elizabeth and that of her great-great-grandmother. Each had shrewd statesmen to guide her : Lord Melbourne during Queen Victoria's earlier years and Sir Winston Churchill in the case of Queen Elizabeth. Each was complemented by a consort who would by forceful personality and intelligence enhance the throne. Like his eminent ancestor, Philip was a foreign prince. And rightly or wrongly because of their alien origin they were at first treated with suspicion by the public on marrying into the royal line.

With Prince Albert the dislike was mutual. An intellectual, he was somewhat scornful of the way the British lived, and to express their resentment the people were hostile to his naturalization as an Englishman. But only the most unfairly biased would deny that his contribution to British monarchy was immense. Certainly for the last decade of his life his was the guiding hand that led Victoria. Happily in his final years he gained the prestige and respect which was due to him. Death deprived him of greater honour and, as Lytton Strachey pointed out, took from the State a man 'grown grey in the service of the nation, virtuous, intelligent and with the unmistakable experience of a whole lifetime of government'.

Prince Philip is from a different mould. To begin with he had the advantage of being reared like a well-to-do Englishman. Without any deliberate effort on his part he quickly ingratiated himself into the goodwill of the people. This is attributable to a spontaneous wit, an extrovert manner, and to the fact that he was tested in battle as a naval officer in the last war.

Perhaps most significant of all is his zest for life, an inquiring mind which genuinely seeks to acquire knowledge and his affable approach to affairs generally. He has the gift of mixing with ordinary folk without impairing the image of royalty. By associating with the lower deck of the Navy, and indeed in other spheres, he has perhaps a more intimate assessment of the way the majority of people think and feel than most Tory Ministers.

Constitutionally he has no status other than as the husband of the Queen. But he has not allowed the vacuum in which he found himself to cause dismay. A less assertive personality might easily have receded into the background of Court life. Yet while respecting the status of the Queen, he has refused to be eclipsed by it. He has carved his own particular niche and in his way has brought a sparkle to monarchy.

An individualist of sprightly mind, on occasions his rather forcible views have not escaped censure. Yet like the distinguished Albert in his own time he has a keener insight into the pattern that the new industrial age should take than many in Britain. Fascinated by modern invention, Prince Philip is concerned that the objective of the modern technical age should be to serve man rather than exploit him. He demonstrates this by personal example; for instance, for many of his engagements he pilots a helicopter to avoid traffic.

Writing his own speeches (and some of the Queen's), he has

achieved the knack of delivering the verbal barb as an amusing sally, without embarrassing the Queen.

His arrival at Buckingham Palace had a traumatic effect on Court officials who spent hours worrying over what he might say. To some people Philip might appear to be iconoclastic but his remarks are often based on harsh truth. Criticism is less prevalent today and like other members of the royal family he has learnt to ignore impertinent intrusion into his private life. He once told a party of newspaper owners: 'I am completely stoic. I now read about myself – especially the ruder remarks – as if I were an animal at a zoo.'

Neither the Queen nor Prince Philip would claim to be intellectuals but both are endowed with humour and good sense, far more praiseworthy qualities for monarchy in these unstable times.

To what degree, if any, he influences the Queen one cannot assess. Doubtless, in the same way as Prince Albert, in private life he exercises his right as the father of the family. Albert went further. 'Albert helped me with the blotting-paper when I signed', revealed Queen Victoria when she was first married. But later he did much more. It is obvious that he was Victoria's confidential adviser, offering the benefit of his erudition and political sagacity, not only to the Queen but to some of her Ministers. Disraeli was emphatic on this point: 'With Prince Albert we have buried our sovereign. This German Prince has governed England for twenty-one years with a wisdom and energy such as none of our kings have ever shown.... If he had outlived some of our "old stagers" he would have given us the blessings of absolute government.'

Could Prince Philip ever achieve such power? One sphere which quickly felt his influence was Buckingham Palace itself. Like Queen Victoria's husband he found certain longstanding practices rather wearisome. For instance, on returning to Buckingham Palace late at night, the Queen cannot simply ring a bell or ask on the house telephone for light refreshment; such requests have to be dealt with by at least four people. And breakfast, by Philip's standards, was even more tedious; the

I

Palace kitchens are too far from the dining room. He therefore started to cook his own meals on an electric frying-pan – a decision which is reminiscent of Rowlandson's cartoon portraying Queen Charlotte frying sprats at an open fire. While Queen Elizabeth may have admired her husband's enterprise she was less enthusiastic over the lingering odours. Meals were served as before.

One wonders when the Queen's husband will be known officially as the Prince Consort. It is solely a matter for the Queen, although Prince Philip has no wish to be created Prince Consort. Prince Albert had to wait patiently for seventeen years before Victoria granted him the style and title. Complaining to his brother, he wrote: 'This ought to have been done . . . at our wedding.' Although the present Queen's husband was for years referred to as Prince Philip this was a misnomer. When on 20 November 1947 George VI conferred upon his son-in-law the title and style of Royal Highness he did not create the Duke of Edinburgh a prince. It was not until 22 February 1957 that the Queen declared that the Duke 'shall henceforth be known as His Royal Highness The Prince Phillip, Duke of Edinburgh'. Until he receives the style Prince Consort, that will be his title.

Soon after the Queen's accession it was suggested that Philip should be elevated to the impressive title of King or King Consort but, of course, lacking the Queen's constitutional powers. An alternative was Prince Royal.

When Queen Elizabeth succeeded her father there was speculation as to whether she would be the last monarch of the House of Windsor. Normally a queen regnant would be the last of her dynasty. Would her heir Prince Charles assume his father's adopted name and begin a new dynasty, the House of Mountbatten? The topic was debated in learned quarters.

At the time of her father's birth the royal family had used no surname since the days of Queen Anne, the last of the reigning Stuarts; for when her successor, the German Princeling who became George I, arrived in London from Hanover he brought no surname. Many years earlier his family had been known variously as Guelph, Este or Wettin, but for generations these had been dispensed with. Until 1917 all members of the British royal family were styled 'Highness'. However, during that year King George v restricted the use of princely styles to children of the monarch and of the monarch's sons but not of his daughters. It was therefore imperative to adopt a surname for the latter. As Britain was then at war with Germany the King decided against continuing Prince Albert's family name – Saxe-Coburg and Gotha – and took the name of Windsor for Queen Victoria's descendants in the male line. It was the desire of the Queen's grandfather that the name would be permanent: 'determined that henceforth our House and Family shall be styled and known as the House of Windsor'.

What he did not anticipate was that the succession might pass to a female. However, on 9 April 1952 Queen Elizabeth ii declared in the Privy Council her 'Will and Pleasure that She and her Children shall be styled and known as the House and Family of Windsor, and Her descendants, other than female descendants who marry, and other descendants, shall bear the name of Windsor'. Yet out of respect for her husband on 8 February 1960 she announced that while she and her children would continue to be known as the House and Family of Windsor, her descendants, other than those entitled to the style and title of Royal Highness and Prince or Princess and families who emerged and their children, should bear the name of Mountbatten-Windsor.

ॐ 9 Household and Housekeeping

The machinery of British monarchy would grind to a halt without the royal household. This has always been so, for originally it was the hub of government. The great officers of State (that is, the ceremonial household as distinct from the personal staff) were the monarch's closest advisers and, by the nature of the executive power exercised by the King, the main administrators.

As an institution, much of the household lives on its faded memories of glory long ago. In the shadowy dawn of kingship the chamberlains were the monarch's personal attendants, but as government grew more complicated they gave advice and administered executive power. Obviously their fortunes were entwined with those of the King. In the long struggle between the sovereigns and their Parliaments from the twelfth to the seventeenth centuries Parliament slowly rejected monarchical power, securing liberty for itself, the Exchequer and the judiciary.

For the household officers there was a return to their early function of assistance in the sovereign's personal affairs, which is more or less the situation today. Before the kings lost the power struggle they frequently chose their intimates to be household officers. But with the ascendency of party government the faction temporarily in control recommended advocates of their own particular policies to be close to the monarch, which meant a replacement of appointees with each successive Liberal and Conservative Government. The practice evoked an outburst from Queen Victoria who in what history now calls the 'Bedchamber Incident' angrily rejected the policy of changing her ladies-in-waiting to meet party demands.

With changing times certain offices became obsolete and others of little use were weeded out. Today Queen Elizabeth II has the service of a compact household, whose decorative titles tend to camouflage their day-to-day duties. Listed are ten units, but only four fulfil their responsibilities within Buckingham Palace. A fifth – the Central Chancery of the Orders of Knighthood – is housed outside. The rest, among which are the medical and eccesiastical sections, are mostly of an advisory nature, and serve in an honorary capacity or are staffed when action demands.

The Queen makes her own choice of household members, of those without political connections; for certain posts today have governmental as well as household duties to carry out. Thus the Treasurer, Comptroller and Vice-Chamberlain (all nominees of the political party in power) act as Government Whips in the House of Commons, and the Captain of the Gentlemen-at-Arms, the Captain of the Yeomen of the Guard and three of the five non-permanent Lords-in-Waiting act as Government Whips in the House of Lords. Only the Lord Chamberlain, Lord Steward, Master of the Horse and the non-political Lords-in-Waiting have, since 1924, been appointed by the personal choice of the sovereign, and this is solely on condition that they do not vote against the government of the day in the House of Lords (of which they are all members).

Almost four hundred people are listed on the household staff: an impressive array. Yet only about one-quarter work full time for the Queen; the remaining appointments are mostly honorary.

With the growth of ministerial responsibility the power of most of the executives has diminished. For instance, the Lord Chancellor, the Lord President of the Council, the Lord Privy Seal and the Secretary of State (an office now divided between a number of Ministers) are purely political posts held by members of the government. The duties of the ancient office of the Lord High Treasurer are today carried out by the Lords Commissioners of the Treasury and those of the Lord High

Admiral, previously fulfilled by the Lords Commissioners of the Admiralty Board, were assumed by the Queen on 1 April 1964. Two other offices – those of the Lord High Steward and Lord High Constable – are now granted for only the single day of a coronation. While none of the great officers of State retains household functions two (the Lord Great Chamberlain and the Earl Marshal) have continuous duties linked with royal ceremonial.

The office of Lord Great Chamberlain began in the reign of Henry I in the twelfth century, and was invested in the father of the first Earl of Oxford and his heirs. In 1387 when the ninth Earl was disgraced he was succeeded by the Earl of Huntingdon who was beheaded in 1400. The Earls of Oxford regained their hereditary right after a lapse of eighty-five years. In 1902 after three centuries of dispute (because the descent passed through the female line) the House of Lords ruled that the office should be jointly held by three families – the Lords Cholmondeley, Ancaster and Lincolnshire and their heirs. They discharge their duties in turn during successive reigns. Fewer duties are now attached to the office, but the holder participates at the coronation and is entrusted with procedure when the Queen visits Parliament. Originally the Lord Great Chamberlain was head of the sovereign's personal household and all royal palaces. A key is the symbol of his office.

The office of Earl Marshal also originated in the reign of Henry I, and has been hereditary in the family of the Duke of Norfolk since 1672. His duties are entirely ceremonial but as titular head of the English College of Arms – the highest authority on medieval traditions – he has a supervisory status. His responsibilities also include arranging the detail of coronations, royal funerals and other State functions and being present when newly created peers are admitted to the House of Lords. His financial reward is a mere twenty pounds, an annual fee fixed in 1483 and defrayed from the rent of a farm in Ipswich.

For centuries the Lord Steward – who carried a white staff to symbolize his authority at State ceremonies – managed the palace below stairs. As such he controlled the catering for State banquets and other forms of royal entertainment, the hiring and dismissal of domestic staff and the payment of all household expenses. Until 1849 (when it was abolished) he was the chief judge of the Court of the Appeals of Westminster which dealt with cases against household staff. His functions are now undertaken by the Master of the Household (an office founded by Prince Albert), who resides at Buckingham Palace. On his staff are specialists, for instance, the Keeper of the Royal Cellars who stocks the royal vaults with wines, liqueurs and cigars.

As the leading dignitary at Court the Lord Steward has been superseded by the Lord Chamberlain. There have been Lord Chamberlains ever since Anglo-Saxon times. As the senior officer of the household he carries a white wand and wears a golden key on his hip on ceremonial occasions. In his many-sided office he is responsible for all Court ceremonial, royal garden parties, and State visits in the United Kingdom. He is a member of the Privy Council.

The Lord Chamberlain's office consists of the Comptroller and his staff, who assist the Lord Chamberlain in supervising the household; the Gentleman Usher of the Black Rod, who summons the Commons to the House of Lords (where he maintains order) when they are required to hear a speech from the throne; other Gentlemen Ushers who attend upon the sovereign; the Constable and Deputy Constable of Windsor Castle; the Ecclesiastical Household; the Marshal of the Diplomatic Corps; Lords-in-Waiting; the Sergeant-at-Arms; the Pages of Honour; the Keeper of the Jewel House, Tower of London; the Master of the Queen's Music; the Poet Laureate; the Art Surveyors; the Bargemaster; and the Keeper of the Queen's Swans.

Years ago when dismissed from office the Lord Chamberlain broke his staff in half, but nowadays it is made to unscrew so that he can keep a portion as a memento. With the death of the sovereign his services automatically cease, although in practice he continues in office for a few months in the new reign. At the funeral he places half his staff upon the coffin.

By tradition the Vice-Chamberlain is the Lord Chamberlain's deputy. But, as in the case of the Treasurer and Comptroller, the connection is purely ceremonial, the appointment being entirely political. He does, however, write for the Queen a daily confidential report of the proceedings in Parliament, When the Queen opens Parliament she is attended by the Treasurer and the Comptroller in the House of Lords. On her return to Buckingham Palace she is received by the Vice-Chamberlain who, like the Lord Chamberlain and the Lord Great Chamberlain, wears a golden key. No one knows the reason for the origin of this practice.

After the Lord Chamberlain and the Lord Steward, the Master of the Horse is the third dignitary at Court. The holder of a distinguished office (the powerful Essex, for example, was the Master for the first Elizabeth), his nominal activities centre on the Queen's stables, which are actually run by his deputy the Chief or Crown Equerry, who has jurisdiction over the other equerries and pages in the royal mews. He provides the horses, carriages and motor cars needed for processions and the daily requirement of the royal family. On State occasions the Master of the Horse rides immediately behind the Queen.

Incidentally, all equerries of the household – regular, extra or honorary – are serving officers. Now there are two regular equerries, who have a continuing role of attendance, as one of them is always in waiting upon the sovereign. They accompany her when she appears in public and their duties vary from knowing the names and background of guests to be presented to securing theatre tickets.

The Keeper of the Privy Purse and Treasurer to the Queen deals with personal payments made from her private resources and with the payment of salaries and wages to her officers and servants. His department consists of the Privy Purse Office, the Treasurer's Office, and the Royal Almonry – an ecclesiastical appointment usually headed by a bishop.

Long ago the members of the female household entertained

the queen regnant or queen consort, conveyed her messages and attended their mistress when she retired to bed and rose in the morning. The senior officer in the Queen's female household is the Mistress of the Robes whose rank is seldom below that of a duchess. Attending Her Majesty on ceremonial and State occasions – when she has the right to ride in a State carriage – she is responsible for the duties of the Ladies-in-Waiting (sometimes known as Ladies and Women of the Bedchamber) who are on daily duty, attending upon the Queen when she goes out in public, dealing with her private correspondence and undertaking personal service.

At one time the Woman of the Bedchamber handed each garment to the Lady of the Bedchamber, who in turn presented it to the Queen. However, these days each is on duty for a fortnight at a time at Buckingham Palace (or wherever the Queen is in residence), making Her Majesty's telephone calls, communicating her instructions, serving as the liaison between the Queen and the outside world. She is often present when the Queen receives visitors.

Up to the twentieth century the Mistress of the Robes was a political appointment, and consequently the holder always quit office with the arrival of a new government. Again at one time the badge of office was a golden key, passing from on appointee to her successor until the tempestuous Sarah, Duchess of Marlborough, Mistress of the Robes to Queen Anne, stubbornly withheld the key. A miniature of the Queen set in pearls has been the symbol of office ever since.

In some ways Elizabeth II is a medieval monarch amid the twentieth-century scene. This pageantry lives through the College of Arms (or Heralds' College) in England and Wales, a corporation of thirteen members; three Kings of Arms, six Heralds, and four Pursuivants. Members of the royal household, they are all appointed by the Crown by Letters Patent under the Great Seal, on the nomination of the Earl Marshal. There have been members ever since the thirteenth century, but they were not constituted into a corporation until 1484; the present corporation was founded in 1555.

The Kings of Arms are Garter, Clarenceux, and Norroy and Ulster. The office of Garter was created in 1415 by Henry v; Garter is both King of Arms of the Most Noble Order of the Garter and Principal King of Arms. Responsible to the Earl Marshal for conducting the ceremonial when a peer is introduced in the House of Lords he also administers the College (incorporated by Richard III) which conducts its affairs from an attractive old London building in the lea of St Paul's Cathedral.

Clarenceux and Norroy were constituted in their offices by the time of Edward III (1327–77), the province of the former comprising all land to the south of the River Trent and that of the latter all land to the north. Two Kings of Arms have the special functions of granting arms by Letters Patent.

The six Heralds are Windsor, Chester, Lancaster, York, Richmond and Somerset, who take precedence according to seniority in office. The four Pursuivants are Rouge Croix, Bluemantle, Rouge Dragon and Portcullis.

As well as verifying and recording arms and genealogies and research in such matters, the Kings of Arms, Heralds and Pursuivants attend upon the sovereign at such ceremonial coronation as State funerals, State openings of Parliament, and ceremonies connected with the Order of the Garter. The duty of making royal proclamations also falls to them.

In Scotland analogous functions are exercised by Lord Lyon King of Arms, so called from the lion rampant, the armorial bearing of the Scottish kings. Under him are three Heralds, Marchmont, Rothesay and Albany, and four Pursuivants, Kintyre, Carrick, Unicorn and Falkland (Pursuivant Extraordinary). The Lyon Court is the only Court of Chivalry in the world and in Scotland adjudicates all disputed claims of succession within clans.

The Officers of Arms in Scotland are not under the jurisdiction of the Earl Marshal. Since 1867 they have been government appointments.

The practice of maintaining bodyguards to protect the monarch is believed to have begun with King Canute (1016–35). The Honourable Corps of Gentlemen-at-Arms is termed the

Queen's 'nearest guard' since it is (and from its inception always has been) the corps in the closest personal attendance upon the sovereign of England. When it was created in 1509 it was composed of fifty 'young nobles gorgeously attired'. Today the strength is twenty-eight Gentlemen (one of whom is the Harbinger, who in the old days went in advance to secure lodgings) and four officers. Under the administrative control of the Lord Chamberlain it attends the Queen on all State occasions, and is present at many Palace functions.

Perhaps the Queen's Yeomen of the Guard are the most picturesque of her decorative bodyguards. They have served English Kings and Queens for four and a half centuries. Although it is the most ancient royal bodyguard and military corps in the world remnants of an even older corps exist in the person of the Sergeants-at-Arms, royal household officials on duty in the Houses of Parliament. Originally the Yeomen protected the monarch by day and night, both at home and abroad, on journeys, on the battlefield and within the Palace walls. They also examined and made the sovereign's bed and these duties are perpetuated in the ranks of Yeoman Bed Goer and Yeoman Bed Hanger. A further duty was to cook the sovereign's food and carry the dishes to his table – a service now symbolized by the Exon-in-Waiting standing behind the Queen at State banquets.

Today the duties are mostly ceremonial and include guard attendance at the reception of foreign dignitaries and Heads of State. Their permanent orderly room is at St James's Palace, where routine duty is carried on by the Clerk of the Cheque and Adjutant. Uniforms are stored in the charge of the resident Wardrobe Keeper.

Contrary to widespread belief the warders of the Tower of London are not Yeomen of the Guard, although they wear a similar uniform. Popularly they are known as 'Beefeaters' – a nickname which had its origin in 1669, when Count Cosimo, Grand Duke of Tuscany, was in England and, writing of the size and stature of 'this magnificent body of men', observed: 'They are great eaters of beef, of which a very large ration is given them daily at Court, and they might be called beef-eaters'. They have their origin in the twelve yeomen young Henry VIII left behind in the Tower when he ceased to reside there permanently. With the Tower no longer a royal palace, the Yeomen became warders – curiously termed 'Extraordinary of the Guard' – and are today in the command of the Constable of the Tower.

In Scotland the Queen's personal bodyguard is the Royal Company of Archers dating from 1676 when it was called His Majesty's Company of Archers. During the visit of George IV to Edinburgh in 1822 it became the King's bodyguard for Scotland. Its ceremonial duties include attendance on the Queen at the Courts held at the Palace of Holyroodhouse.

There are also regiments of the Regular Army which guard the Queen and the metropolis of London: the Household Cavalry and the Foot Guards. The Household Cavalry consists of the Life Guards and the 'Blues and Royals', each of which is an armoured corps regiment but has a mounted squadron for State duties in London. The Life Guards were founded by troops of the Royalist Cavaliers who fought for Charles I during the Civil War, while the 'Blues and Royals' or 'Blues' are descended from Cromwell's Heavy Regiment of Horse. Both were incorporated into the standing army in 1661, became the monarch's bodyguard, and were held responsible for his protection. In April 1969 the Royal Horse Guards were amalgamated with the Royal Dragoons; hence the name 'Blues and Royals'.

Colonels and lieutenant-colonels of the Household Cavalry enjoy the exclusive privilege of performing the duties of Goldstick-in-Waiting and Silverstick-in-Waiting, appointments which originated in 1528 following the conspiracy against the life of Henry VIII. As the royal person was in danger one of the King's captains was ordered to wait next to the King, carrying an ebony staff with a gold head, and another principal officer carrying an ebony staff with a silver head waited near the captain to afford him occasional relief. These officers were with the King continuously except in the royal bedchamber.

Gradually these duties were handed down to the Household

Cavalry. Nowadays the colonels of the Life Guards and of the 'Blues and Royals' fulfil in turn the function of Goldstick for a month at a time. Lieutenant-colonels take duty as Silverstick in a similar way. At State ceremonials they stand immediately on the right hand of or behind the Queen, according to circumstances.

The Foot Guards of the Household Troops consist of five regiments: the Grenadier Guards, founded in 1656 from among officers and men who had remained loyal to the royalist cause; the Coldstream Guards, originally formed by Cromwell from companies of the New Model Army, but later supporting the King and helping to restore the monarchy; the Scots Guards, reformed in 1660 from a regiment raised in 1642 by the Marquis of Argyll; the Irish Guards introduced in 1900 at the instigation of Queen Victoria; and the Welsh Guards, set up by order of George V in 1915.

The royal income is derived from the Queen's private property (Sandringham in Norfolk and Balmoral in Aberdeenshire), the hereditary revenues of the Duchy of Lancaster, and an annual income – called the Civil List – granted by Parliament to meet the cost of maintaining the royal household.

Against the cynical who claim that the institution and machinery of monarchy are a drain on the public purse one could argue that not only is the monarchy self-sufficient but it presents the Treasury with a surplus. This is because of the deal between the early Georges and Parliament. Until 1760 the monarchs had to provide for the payment of such civil expenses as the salaries of judges, ambassadors, civil servants and the expenses of the royal palaces and households. For this purpose he had available hereditary revenues made up of income from Crown lands and from other sources such as prerogative rights of treasure trove, royal mines, royal fish and swans, and from certain ecclesiastical sources such as tithes or the income of bishoprics during a vacancy.

In addition Parliament granted the monarch the income from

some customs duties, from certain assigned taxes (for example, those on beer, ale and cider) and the Post Office revenues.

However, when Britain's population grew so did the cost of government. The income from all these sources proved inadequate and when George III became King he turned over to the government most of the hereditary revenues and received in return an annual grant (Civil List) of £800,000, out of which he had to continue to pay royal expenditure of a personal nature and also the salaries of the Civil Service, judges, ambassadors and certain pensions. This sum in turn proved insufficient, and in 1830 the extraneous charges on the Civil List were removed and the amount of the grant was reduced.

But George III and George IV got the best of the bargain. George IV, whose ten-year reign has been described as crammed with little but adulteries, lies and debts (he and his brothers squandered vast sums gambling and drinking), persuaded Parliament to grant him an additional £500,000. Hence the Duke of Wellington's complaint that the Royal Family were 'the damndest millstone about the neck of any government that could be imagined'. It was not just the debts which irked the Duke. Like his father George IV's behaviour was sometimes odd; he suffered on occasions from the delusion that he had led a murderous cavalry charge at Waterloo. Turning to the Duke he would ask: 'Did I not do so, Arthur?' and the Duke would tactfully reply: 'I have often heard your Majesty relate the incident.'

In fairness monarchy was still shackled with heavy financial commitments. It was not until Queen Victoria's reign that the sovereign was finally relieved of the cost of the last item of governmental responsibility: the secret service. In return the Queen permitted Parliament to take the hereditary revenue from the Crown lands for life, save those of the Duchy of Cornwall (which belongs to the heir apparent) and the Duchy of Lancaster. Thus Victoria rid the monarchy of the anxieties of government expenses and fixed an annual income for herself.

According to law the title of the Crown lands – the inception of which began at least in Anglo-Saxon times – stays with the monarch. Thus one of the first acts of Queen Elizabeth II was to inform Parliament that she surrendered her hereditary revenues and put herself 'at the disposal of the House of Commons with regard to the Civil List'. And so during the first six months of her accession (in 1952) a Parliamentary Committee, after consulting the Keeper of the Privy Purse and other household officials, recommended an annual payment of £475,000 for the rest of her reign.

In the years following the Second World War the Civil List, which had been fixed at £410,000 in 1937, proved insufficient to meet rising costs. The government therefore undertook to relieve the Civil List of the cost of certain services, including the upkeep of Buckingham Palace gardens, the salaries of the Yeomen of the Guard and the Gentlemen-at-Arms, and also expenditure on fuel, light, telephones and telegrams. In addition the cost of the wages of industrial staff engaged in maintaining the royal palaces was removed from the Civil List, for which an adjustment was made in 1952.

Together with annuities for certain members of the royal family it was expected that this would suffice throughout the reign, but soaring inflation made the sums too meagre. After an inquiry a Select Committee published its findings in November 1971 – much against Bagehot's advice years earlier. 'When there is a Select Committee on The Queen', he wrote, 'the charm of royalty will be gone. Its mystery is its life. We must not let in daylight upon magic.'

The report caused discord among the politicians; whereas the Conservatives favoured a bigger Civil List, Labour and Liberal Members, while agreeing on the need to provide more adequately for the Queen and her family, preferred to create a Department of the Crown under a Permanent Secretary answerable to Parliament. In the end the Conservative opinion prevailed. The Civil List rose to £980,000 a year for the Queen and her household and the annuities were increased. But a royal trustee will now report on royal expenditure once every ten years.

Whatever is said of the cost of maintaining British monarchy the Hanoverian deal with Parliament has turned out to be most lucrative for the Treasury. In 1970–1 Crown estate revenues, mostly from landed property, amounted to £5,583,000 and the figure is still rising. As well as valuable property and agricultural land there is offshore dredging for mineral wealth and other revenue from stone and gravel, fisheries, oyster beds and wrecks, and whales and sturgeon caught in British waters. Then there is treasure trove, the property of anyone who dies without leaving kin or claimants upon the estate, gold or silver mines, the right to search for oil in the United Kingdom, and income from certain ecclesiastical sources.

The system of payment to Queen Elizabeth is based on 'negotiable receipts' drawn on the Exchequer. Every three months the Paymaster-General sends chits to the Keeper of the Privy Purse amounting to one-quarter of the Civil List. The income is not so enormous when it is considered that, as one item alone, the Queen entertains something like thirty thousand guests each year. True, the Queen pays no income tax on any of the financial provisions from the State.

When income tax was introduced in 1842 at 7d. in the pound, Queen Victoria, as a public-spirited gesture, voluntarily exposed her income to taxation. Edward VII imitated his mother, but when Lloyd George, Chancellor of the Exchequer, presented King George V's Civil List to Parliament he proposed that the voluntary payment of income tax should be abandoned since he considered that the Civil List was not a salary but an allowance made to the sovereign towards the maintenance of the dignity of the Crown, the Civil List being either adequate or inadequate for the purpose for which it was granted. This recommendation was duly approved by Parliament.

Taxation of the Queen's private estates is provided for in the Crown Private Estates Act of 1862. A sovereign's estate is not liable to death duty, but this does not apply to other members of the royal family who also pay income tax.

40 The *Liber Regalis*, the fourteenth-century Order of Service may have been produced in 1382 for the crowning of Anne of Bohemia.

41 *(Below)* Balmoral, where the Queen is laird, in the grip of winter.

42 (*Above*) The west front of Sandringham, the vast Norfolk estate where agriculture and the breeding of bloodstock has been developed by the Queen and Prince Philip on a sound economic basis. The estate includes some of Britain's most valuable land.

43 (*Below*) Queen Elizabeth stays at Holyroodhouse in Edinburgh each summer to fulfil official functions. Centuries ago the Augustinian Abbey of Holyrood was founded here.

44 A glimpse of the Queen's Gallery at Buckingham Palace. These and other treasures at Windsor Castle, and elsewhere, have been collected by sovereigns since Henry VIII. It is the only royal collection to survive in Europe.

45 (*Above*) Buckingham
Palace – the Queen's m
official home – stands i
grounds once occupied
a smaller house bought
George III. However,
original red-brick mans
was too modest for his
flamboyant son, George
who instructed his arch
John Nash, to extend i

46 Windsor Castle, w
the Queen and her fam
like to spend their wee
is one of the most disti
homes in the world. It
began as a fortress erec
by William the Conqu
to overawe the Anglo-

47 The Queen and Prince Philip relaxing on the Balmoral estate. However, even when the Court is away from London, there is still the inexorable flow of official documents and State business to cope with.

49 Queen Elizabeth with
her family at the time of her
Silver Wedding anniversary;
(left to right) Prince Charles
(heir to the throne), Prince
Edward, the Queen, the
Duke of Edinburgh, Prince
Andrew and Princess Anne.

8 (*Left*) A bedroom of
another age at Windsor –
the royal home beloved by
the Queen's Hanoverian
ancestor, George III. In
his castle of poignant
memories, one can visualise
that pathetic monarch
aimlessly wandering its
corridors and rooms in his
madness.

50 Resplendent in gold,
white and red, the Throne
Room at Buckingham
Palace is one of the State
Apartments. Beneath an
ornate canopy stand the
thrones occupied by the
Queen and Prince Philip at
official functions.

51 The Chair of State in the Queen's Robing Room at the Palace of Westminster. The cloth at the rear of the dais was embroidered with the Royal Arms and Queen Victoria's monogram by the Royal School of Needlework in 1856.

52 The White Drawing Room at Buckingham Palace. Here a spring swings a huge mirror and cabinet exposing the secret door to a room where the Queen and members of the Royal Family can retire for a while during exhausting receptions.

Based on annual salary alone it is more costly to maintain a monarchy than it is to maintain a presidency as in the United States. For example however, the cost of a presidency escalates in other ways, with elections and conventions taking place every few years. It could also be argued that the Scandinavian and Dutch monarchies are even more expensive than their British counterpart when one compares the relative smallness of their populations.

In any event, the intrinsic value of the British monarchy far exceeds the cost. Under the British system the Head of State cannot be tainted by the equivalent of a Watergate scandal; moreover, there can be no Hitler or Mussolini *while the Queen is true to her coronation oath.* By the very character of her office Queen Elizabeth is a stabilizing factor and the permanent trustee of the constitution. Just as important she is the embodiment of the continuity and unity of Britain's national life. As such she represents the people as a whole, not merely one section. In contrast a president, whose tenure of office is always prescribed, is merely the choice of those who voted for him. He can never be a truly national representative in every sense.

Indeed, as the hereditary monarch Queen Elizabeth fills a niche which no president could ever occupy. She is the visible link with the nation's centuries-old history, being a direct descendant of those Kings and Queens who helped their country to grow from an insignificant island nation into a major power. That is why the British prefer dualism : a Head of State and a Head of Government. With a changing public opinion a Head of Government is inevitably replaced, sooner or later, by a political opponent. To achieve continuity of national life and the unity of national purpose, there must therefore be a permanent figure. These two institutions cannot be supplied efficiently by one person. There are countries where one person is appointed to both offices, but it can result in a dangerous situation – dictatorship. Constitutional monarchy is on a higher plane when it remains apart from the friction and antagonism of politics and devotes itself to the unity and continuity of the State.

The continuity of the monarchy inspires most Britons,

consciously or not, with a sense of the continuity of national life through a long and eventful past and in the centuries to come. The monarchy as it exists in Britain gives stability to British political forms and social structure. It is a bulwark against revolutionary dreams but at no time is it a conservative institution. It has encouraged change, and it has changed itself in the process. This is one reason why it has survived so long.

The steadying – and perhaps tranquilizing – effect of the monarchy has been evident in Queen Elizabeth's reign during social revolution and especially when the nation wilted under the trauma of losing the Empire. Continuing assuredly amid the magnificence of her ancestors the monarch has helped to conceal the reality of a changing Britain.

In such a climate republicanism seems to have little chance to root. There were sporadic outbursts last century; the poet Shelley vehemently wrote: 'Oh, that the free world stamp the impious name of king into the dust!'

The republican movement began to thrive among middle-class radicals and the working class. The Chartists confidently, yet wrongly, assumed that when the workers secured political power the monarchy would disappear with the House of Lords and other relics of the Middle Ages. In the 1860s, when Queen Victoria became a recluse after her husband's death, republican sentiment hardened, partly because of the Queen's own attitude; people resented her readiness to accumulate a fortune out of the Civil List without fulfilling any apparent function. During his Mediteranean tour in 1868–9 Prince Edward wrote to his mother from Egypt stressing that 'we are living in radical times and the more people see the sovereign, the better it is for the people and the country'. Ostensibly Victoria was more concerned with her Scots ghillie, John Brown, than with pomp and pageantry. That is why the Queen became the object of scurrilous pamphlets and was scathingly referred to as Mrs John Brown.

Led by Charles Bradlaugh, some Members of Parliament sympathized with the republican cause. Bradlaugh published a pamphlet called *An impeachment of the House of Brunswick*, writing that it was his 'earnest desire that the present Prince of Wales should never dishonour this country by becoming King'. Involved in baccarat scandals and the divorce court the behaviour of the Prince, who was nicknamed contemptuously 'Guelpho the Gay', made matters worse.

The fall of Napoleon III and the proclamation of the French Third Republic in September 1870 also stimulated republican feeling in Britain. There were mass demonstrations and republican clubs mushroomed in most of the big towns.

But the republican fever subsided with the illness of the Prince of Wales and the subsequent outburst of public rejoicing on his recovery. The Queen returned from obscurity. She won the allegiance of the powerful middle class. To the majority of her subjects she was seen as a maternal figure, the symbol of the greatness of Britain and the Empire. By the time of her death she had moulded the shape of royalty for the new century; withdrawn from government (though she herself had exasperated her Ministers), but deeply representative of and identified with the people.

In Britain any dream of ejecting the monarch for a president faded. Not so in many parts of Europe. Since the end of the First World War most of the monarchies have been ousted by republics. But has the change proved beneficial? It has been claimed that the outcome has been acute disorder, that the last half-century has been the most agitated period in Europe since the French Revolution. Much has happened to make one wonder if republics have been the wiser choice.

In a republic men must put their faith and aspirations into a national flag, a piece of bunting, but this is no counterpart to flesh and blood, especially in the form of a hereditary monarch who is the symbol of union and the gift of human fellowship, of the art of tolerating differences and of the gift of weaving differences together in a common agreement which is all the better for the differences. This is the greatest height of British constitutional monarchy, and it is the greatest and surest pledge of continuance.

Advocates of republicanism can argue that hereditary

K*

monarchy cannot safeguard against an inability to perform the duties of sovereign. No doubt they have George III in mind when during 1787 he dismounted from his carriage in Windsor Great Park and addressed an oak tree as the King of Prussia. But there is always a royal substitute.

At the same time there is no guarantee that the president of a republic possesses soundness of mind. One can quote, for instance, the unfortunate case of Paul Eugène Deschanel. Elected tenth President of the French Third Republic in January 1920 he was compelled to resign office in the following September because of what has been euphemistically described as neurotic troubles.

Any criticism of hereditary monarchy can be countered by the contention that the politicians of any country do not represent the quintessence of intellect of their respective nations. The devotees of republicanism cannot guarantee that a republican system assures the emergence of a Head of State of finer calibre (it rarely produced women candidates) than does a monarchist country.

Beyond all this there is the sentimental and emotional appeal of monarchy. The British constitutional system is made of something more than cold reason and commonplace policies. It demands the colours that have embellished it down the years – royal purple and imperishable scarlet. Ticker-tape and the confetti of torn-up telephone directories are poor substitutes for medieval pageantry. The occasions when the monarch is on parade are times when national emotions and the rivalries of politics are centred on the sovereign. These events spread out the rich tapestry of the past, imposing for an hour or two colourful ritual on a twentieth-century scene which is gradually growing more drab. Like the long British monarchic line these displays of pageantry – in some instances born as long ago as Norman times – are spectacular proof to the British that a great past is a solid foundation for the future.

It has been said with some justification that human nature craves for colour and romance if only to escape for a few moments from the dull environment that so often surrounds it.

The Roman Catholic Church, with its ancient ritual and the mystery of its festivals, has long been aware of this. So, too, have most British Socialists. King George v feared that if the Socialists ever atttained power his descendants had only a remote chance of ever succeeding to the throne. Most Socialist politicians have the good sense to realize that, as the symbol of the nation's past, Queen Elizabeth appeals not only to the head but to the heart. When one glances round the world and sees the nations which have severed that link with monarchy, one feels no burning anxiety to imitate them.

The perceptive Bagehot had his own way of expressing it. 'Royalty', he observed, 'is a government in which the attention of the nation is concentrated on one person doing interesting actions. A Republic is a government in which that attention is divided between many, who are all doing uninteresting actions. Accordingly, so long as the human heart is strong and the human reason weak, Royalty will be strong because it appeals to diffused feeling, and Republics weak because they appeal to understanding.'

§ 10 Royal Homes and Treasures

Down the centuries much of the nation's history has been enacted in the royal palaces. And though many have disappeared – the victims of fire or ravaged by decay – there is still an impressive array to reawaken the past. Queen Elizabeth herself has three official residences, which some might argue is more than enough for her needs. Yet by the standards of her Tudor namesake, the accommodation of the House of Windsor is extremely paltry. Elizabeth I had the choice of fourteen palaces and could rightly bemoan that she was not so well served as her medieval predecessors.

This has not lessened the prestige of modern British monarchy. Her Majesty is so widely known throughout the world that her address is simply *Buckingham Palace*. In London this is her official residence : a combination of private quarters, royal offices and the venue of State ceremonial. To thousands of tourists each year it is magnetic; to the British it is the focal point of national jubilation or sadness. The curious thing is that while Buckingham Palace is such a popular attraction and a symbol of national stability, it has never wholly endeared itself to the royal inhabitants; over the years they have subjected it to liberal abuse or indifference. William IV attempted various ruses to avoid living there. Queen Victoria wrote querulously that the exterior was 'a disgrace' (even underlining the word to give royal emphasis). For years after her adored Prince Consort's death she deserted it, and Edward VII with usual forthrightness christened it 'the sepulchre'. But maybe it constantly reminded him of the heavy parental demands in childhood and the frustrating vacuum in which his mother left him as heir apparent. And coming to more recent times George v, it was rumoured, had designs on forsaking 'Buck House' for Kensington Palace. The mass of maligned masonry has even been hysterically criticized as a 'monstrous insult upon the nation'.

For various reasons the British monarchy has on occasions hinted at possible departure. Even in November 1969 Prince Philip, questioned on American television, remarked: 'We go into the red, I think, next year. . . . We may have to move into smaller premises, who knows?' The fact is that, for many decades, royalty have consistently lived in Buckingham Palace.

The site of the Palace first crept into history when James i sponsored a scheme to produce raw silk. Some 30,000 trees were duly planted but royal initiative went wrong: the planners chose black mulberries instead of the white mulberries on which the silkworm feeds. Today a solitary gnarled tree in the spacious grounds of Buckingham Palace is a lone memento of this abortive scheme. A brighter and more lucrative future for the Mulberry Garden lay in the ill repute it next gained as a place of licentious pleasure and night-club life. John Evelyn in 1654 complained that it was 'now the only place of refreshment about the town for persons of the best quality to be exceedingly cheated at'. He also noted with disfavour 'how women began to paint themselves, formerly a most ignominious thing, and used only by prostitutes'. His fellow diarist, Samuel Pepys, also censured 'a very silly place, worse than Spring Gardens, and but little company, and those of a rascally, whoring, roguing sort of people, only a wilderness, that is somewhat pretty, but rude'.

Nearby a number of mansions rose and fell and were rebuilt. Finally in 1705 John Sheffield, Duke of Buckingham and Normanby, erected the finest private mansion near London, Buckingham House. Not far from Parliament in Westminster, the mansion also afforded the Duke the benefit of a rural estate. There was 'a little wilderness full of blackbirds and nightingales' beneath the library windows.

Buckingham's third and final wife was the odd, illegitimate

daughter of James II. Her silly eccentricities and the snobbery that sprang from her royal connection earned her the name of 'Princess Buckingham'. On the anniversary of the momentous day her father fled the country the ladies of her household were ordered to be suitably attired as if in mourning, and, although ironically it would one day be a Hanoverian home, Buckingham House became a rendezvous for ineffectual Jacobite intrigue.

As Prince of Wales, George III in 1723 expressed his wish to acquire the mansion but the Duchess, by now a widow, revelled in informing the 'Little Captain' that 'all His Majesty's revenue cannot purchase a place so fit for them, nor for less a sum'. Her inflated selling price of £60,000 brought negotiations to an abrupt end. But in 1762, after her death, George III had no difficulty inducing the Duke's illegitimate son, who inherited the property, to sell for £21,000. The King's object was to seek royal seclusion for his wife, the shy Queen Charlotte, from the glare of Court life at St James's. The congenial atmosphere of the mansion, renamed the Queen's House in 1775, was so much to the King's liking that it became the setting of royal family life. Everywhere Germanic discipline prevailed; everyone adhered rigidly to strict etiquette. If a room was occupied by a member of the family and the door was open no one dared pass until it was shut. To knock on the Queen's door was akin to sacrilege; the handle had to be rattled instead.

The King made alterations and additions to the house (at once evoking criticism), the most striking innovation being the magnificent library, the contents of which were donated to the British Museum on the sovereign's death.

It was in the Queen's House that Charlotte bore the fourteen children upon whom the King imposed his harsh (some might even say sadistic) discipline. A contemporary account reveals, 'Princess Sophia told me once that she had seen her two eldest brothers, when they were boys of thirteen and fourteen, held by their arms to be flogged like dogs, with a long whip'.

At the Queen's House George III tried in vain to regain the royal powers which the first two Georges had in their apathy ceded to the politicians. He had been prodded by his mother since childhood to win back the royal prerogatives of earlier monarchs, and in the secrecy of his domestic retreat fostered political intrigue, through the instrument of the 'King's friends', fed on bribery and sycophancy. He gained some measure of success, breaking up the Whig oligarchy, but the fate of monarchy had already been sealed; democracy had tightened the grip which it would never again allow to relax. Wilkes and Liberty, and the raucous cries of the mobs, sounded the limitations of monarchical rights. As the London rioters went on their rampage, the indignant King actually hoped that they would attack his home so that he could charge the rabble 'at the head of his Guards'.

Over the centuries the Palaces of Westminster, Whitehall and St James's had been the official London homes of England's Kings and Queens. Buckingham House did not become an official royal residence until the Prince Regent had succeeded his father. This corpulent wastrel, who could never curb his passion for spending generous sums of public money on fantastic building projects, extracted £200,000 from Parliament to 'repair and mend' Buckingham House. Instead it turned out to be a drastic remodelling job by his friend and protégé, John Nash. Gradually the cost more than trebled, for George IV was bent on having a palace, not merely a mansion. Parliament's indignant protest that the 'Crown of England does not require such splendour' failed to dampen royal ardour. At one period as many as a thousand workmen were active, often labouring at night by candlelight. Ironically, George never lived to reside in his Pimlico Palace, as it was sometimes described. He died and Nash, now deprived of his royal patron, was quickly dismissed.

William IV, who succeeded his brother George, found the building so objectionable that when fire gutted the Palace of Westminster, he tried to induce Parliament to move into Buckingham Palace. When they declined he offered it as barracks for the Guards. Disgruntled he at last settled in himself. At first Victoria, his niece and successor, did not share his disinclination. To everyone's astonishment she readily chose Buckingham Palace as her official home despite its inadequacies.

Until recent times the Palace plumbing was notorious. In Victoria's day only a fraction of the lavatories functioned, and the effluent from one scattered outside her dressing-room window. Furthermore, a sewer beneath the Palace occasionally oozed through into the kitchens. The installation of a hot water pipe 'for the supply of Her Majesty's movable bath and for the bedroom', made life more tolerable.

And when after some ten years she complained that the residence was too small, Parliament had another wing erected to form the fourth side round a central courtyard. As if to avenge themselves on George IV the politicians sold his grandiose Royal Pavilion in Brighton to help pay for it, and transferred some of the gorgeous fireplaces, mirrors and other fixtures to the State Rooms. To make way for the new wing Nash's decorative gateway, the Marble Arch, was transferred to the north-east entrance to Hyde Park and gave its name to that part of London.

Life in the Palace was at times marred by the bickering over Prince Albert's precedence. The Queen's uncles were not prepared to yield to 'a paper Royal Highness'. Argument finally exploded in 1843 at the wedding in Buckingham Palace of Princess Augusta of Cambridge to the Grand Duke of Mecklenburg-Strelitz. Victoria's irate Uncle Ernest, now King of Hanover, deliberately set out to eclipse the Consort.

In a letter to his brother Albert described this rumbustious incident.

It almost came to a fight with the King. He insisted on having the place at the altar, where we stood. He wanted to drive me away, and, against all custom, he wanted to accompany Victoria and lead her. I was to go behind him. I was forced to give him a strong punch and drive him down a few steps, where the First Master of Ceremonies took him and led him out of the Chapel. We had a second scene, where he would not allow me to sign the register with Victoria. He laid his fist on the book. We manoeuvred round the table and Victoria had the book handed to her across the table. Now the table was between us and he could see what was being done. After a third trial to force Victoria to do what he commanded, but in vain, he left the party in great wrath. Since then, we let him go, and happily, he fell over some stones in Kew and damaged some ribs.

The Consort's death brought about the dust-sheet phase at the Palace. The Queen lived mostly at Windsor or Osborne and on the odd occasions that she returned, usually for a State function, Albert's evening clothes were laid out each night.

Of the long cavalcade of personalities who have stayed at Buckingham Palace, one of the most unconventional was the Shah of Persia to whom Victoria lent the Palace in 1873 and who brought with him his harem. But other aspects of the visit, such as the roasting of lambs with cooking tripods that burnt holes in the carpets, provoked the Queen's annoyance. Accounts of the Shah's nocturnal escapades, his disinclination to visit the Palace lavatories and the staging of a prize fight in the grounds failed to excite royal amusement. Far more startling was the alleged murder of a member of the Shah's party with a bow-string.

Buckingham Palace burst into life again with the festive nights of Edward vii. To this day nineteen of his hats and an impressive collection of umbrellas survive in the anteroom of his one time study.

King George v's consort Queen Mary appears to have been the only person to enthuse over Buckingham Palace. Certainly during her years there she took more than a passing interest. Her economies, due to her natural frugality, were almost legendary, yet the story that in the First World War she had a coat made from the skins of rats caught in the Palace must be treated as hyperbole. One innovation was her system of lockers, each bearing the name of a member of the household. Here she stored the articles she bought when opening fêtes and similar functions, and subsequently presented them as Christmas or birthday presents.

Most notable of all was the artistic face-lift which she gave the Palace by systematically cataloguing and rearranging the treasures. It was she who supervised the redecorating of the twelve magnificent state rooms and the balcony room (from which the royal family step on to the celebrated balcony to face the crowds). Modernization of the office and kitchens, as well as the introduction of an efficient system of plumbing can also be attributed to her.

The general design of Buckingham Palace has changed little over the last century. There are three main storeys, called the ground, the principal and the bedroom floors. The grand state rooms and their spacious corridors (which have been converted into highly embellished anterooms) take up virtually half the space; one quarter is devoted to Crown and household offices, and most of the remainder comprises the private quarters of the Queen, her family and her household.

An air of grandeur and opulence, together with chandeliered brilliance, pervades the major state apartments in which Elizabeth II holds Court. There are the Throne Room (radiant in white, gold and red), the State Dining Room (with its enormous dining table over eight feet wide and when extended eighty-one feet long), the State Ballroom (now used for investitures and the more grandiose state banquets), Nash's eye-catching five-bay-windowed Music Room (where guests are presented to the Queen before a state banquet), the Blue Drawing Room (intended by Nash to be a ballroom), the Green Drawing Room, and the White Drawing Room (normally the setting for royal christenings and wedding receptions). In each corner of this exquisite white and gold apartment stand identical ebony china cabinets, yet if a hidden spring is pressed one cabinet and its enormous mirror swing away exposing a secret door of the royal closet. Here the Queen and other members of the royal family can retreat unobtrusively for a while at exhausting receptions.

No one as yet has agreed on the precise number of rooms at Buckingham Palace. But the count has been fixed at 602. Not all the rooms are in daily use, but no items are dust-sheeted. Each day, shortly after dawn, a corps of women descends on the Palace to dust and clean more than one and a half miles of white-painted, red-carpeted corridors as well as the rooms. In this labyrinth people, even Queen Mary, have been known to lose themselves. Some of the corridors are more than twenty feet wide and ranging up to 240 feet in length and they have been transformed into anterooms to accommodate some of the royal treasures. The cleaners are equipped with a variety of brushes, some of which are peculiar to Buckingham Palace, to cope with the high ornate ceilings.

Then there are the footmen, porters, pages and kitchen personnel – a staff commensurate with that of a big hotel. There are no surplus staff. Indeed Prince Philip, like Prince Albert, has effected strict economies. Gone are the days of lavish extravagance when, for instance, servants and trades-people benefited from household laxity. While going through the Palace housekeeping accounts Prince Albert was appalled to discover that, because an order had not been cancelled, two thousand coloured candles had been delivered daily since a ball held eight years earlier. For the domestic staff candles were a coveted perquisite, for after they had been once lit and extinguished, the candles were discarded. At the end of a function these 'Palace ends', as they were called, were snatched from sconces by footmen who obtained high prices for them in the shops.

At Buckingham Palace a dozen men do nothing else but clean the hundreds of windows throughout the year, and one man, from the staff of a Kensington firm, is permanently seconded to wind and regulate the many clocks. Upholsterers and carpet experts constantly maintain the furnishings, and electricians replace some two thousand light bulbs in daily use.

Dress has been one way of effecting household economy. Footmen (who also serve as waiters), porters and pages once wore capitivating gold-braided livery of scarlet and blue. But during the last war, to minimize the laundering of shirt fronts and stiff collars, they were supplied with blue uniforms of battle-dress style. The letters 'ER' in gold braid adorn the left-hand breast pocket. Pages now wear dark blue tail-coats and footmen red ones.

Not even the royal family has evaded the snags caused by the drift from domestic service. In earlier reigns service at the Palace meant unbroken family links, but nowadays most of the staff come from employment exchanges. The loosening of the old ties has inevitably led to trade unionism. To his consternation in 1946 the Queen's father was confronted for the first time with serious dissension among his domestic staff. The social revolution which had marked his reign even invaded the Palace itself. In prewar days domestic staff had worked on alternate days; after the war, owing to staff shortages, hours were long and erratic. A porter then pioneered a Palace branch of the Civil Service Union and the King accepted it, yielding to the pressure of the times.

Yet few servants, if any, would deny that the Queen (who knows many of her servants) is not an attentive employer. The existence of a Royal Household Social Club would have been prohibited before her father's reign. No servant could even address Queen Victoria, for that was the prerogative of a lady-in-waiting or a household official. There is the classic instance when a hot cinder exploded on to the Queen's skirt as she dozed before the fire in the Bow Room. Warning Her Majesty, a maid was curtly chided for impertinence. Nowadays etiquette is if anything, more pronounced below stairs among the servants' ranks themselves, where the rules of authority and precedence are paramount. Senior and junior members are even segregated in different dining rooms. Again, clerical staff dine apart.

These days the living quarters of the domestic staff are beyond reproach. Not so in the Victorian era when they could hope for nothing better than cramped conditions in cold attic or basement dormitories, with about a dozen persons in each. Gambling, drinking and licentious behaviour were commonplace when the staff were off duty. Walls have now been constructed to form private bedrooms.

Banquets at Buckingham Palace are now less frequent than in less stringent times, but all adhere to a traditional ritual. Major banquets take place in the State Ballroom with its massive Gobelin tapestries portraying the story of Janus and the Golden Fleece. Six rose-crystalled chandeliers shed their glitter over the splendid scene.

The routine is always the same on the day of the banquet. In the morning the staff of the Silver Pantry lay white linen table-cloths, then the Yeoman of the glass and china pantry super-vises the arranging of the dishes. The degree of importance of the function will determine if this will be the celebrated gold plate. Under the watchful eye of the Yeoman of the Silver Pantry, the cutlery is next set out, traditionally known as 'laying up'. The forks are no longer placed with the prongs down – a former odd custom originating when, in an irate moment, one of the Hanoverian Georges banged his fist on an upturned fork. Another George bending a gold knife when vainly trying to cut a pippin, testily asked for a steel knife. Since that day the guests have received gold and steel knives with the dessert.

All the gold plate is in the care of the Yeoman of the Gold Pantry. Set against rich red baize, these gorgeous pieces: salvers, flagons, loving cups, and the plaque called Achilles' Shield, are lifted on to stout tables arranged around the room. Now comes a profusion of flowers. The Queen has long since approved the menus, which are printed in French.

As the function draws near the footmen prepare themselves, donning their livery of gold-braided scarlet coats, knee-breeches and buckled shoes. Maybe extra footmen have had to be hired; apart from their fee, they will be entitled to dinner and the choice of a bottle of beer or a double whisky. Perhaps one can detect an element of showmanship in the Queen's procession. Escorted by members of her family and household staff, Her Majesty meets the waiting guests in the White Draw-ing Room, then heads the procession through the most important state apartments, all connected with lofty Spanish mahogany doors mounted on ormolu and fitted with mirrors to catch again the spaciousness and grandeur. When the Queen and her guests are seated there begins a marathon exercise which taxes the stamina of the hardiest footman. Because Buckingham Palace was never planned as a comprehensive whole from the outset the royal kitchens are separated from the ballroom by at least a quarter of a mile of corridors and stone-stepped passageways. Years ago the footmen had to maintain a steady trot, hoping that the food would not arrive cold at the meal table. Queen Victoria's consort lamented, 'Food always tastes so much better in small houses'. Fortunately electrically heated trolleys and electrically heated plates in adjacent serving rooms now help to counter the problem.

While dinner is in progress a military string orchestra entertains the guests from the musicians' gallery, then the meal ends with a royal ritual. Gaily clad in Highland dress the Queen's pipers march into the ballroom, and for a while there is the shrill skirling of pipes around the enormous tables.

For most of the year the Queen and her family live at Buckingham Palace, During that time several dining rooms function daily. Meals for the royal family are prepared in the kitchen nearly half a mile of corridors away from their private dining room.

Although the Queen's father did his utmost to restrict expenditure, on inspecting the Privy Purse accounts Treasury officials noted that the Palace kitchens and dining rooms exceeded their budgets. Responding in a manner which the House of Commons might well copy the King allowed the Master of the Household to call in the managing director of London's Savoy Hotel to reduce costs. The salaries of junior staff members were increased but henceforth meals had to be paid for. Chits had also to be signed by everyone for morning coffee and afternoon tea. But it was still a struggle to cope with budgets. Indeed King George vi had at times to dip into his own private coffers to finance the institution of monarchy.

Buckingham Palace, like Windsor Castle and the Palace of

Holyroodhouse in Edinburgh, is an official residence. The State defrays the cost of maintaining the structures but the running costs and the expenditure involved in entertaining numerous guests is borne by the Queen out of her Civil List. But for a while even she had to help meet expenditure out of her private means. Balmoral and Sandringham are her private residences, and she is wholly responsible for their upkeep.

In recent years Windsor has become increasingly popular with the Queen and the royal family. It has long been traditional for the Court to assemble there for three or four weeks at Easter and for about one week for Ascot in June. But now it has ousted Sandringham as the setting at Christmas time. The Queen and Prince Philip, seeking privacy and an escape from intrusion, now spend most weekends at Windsor. It offers a rural backwater yet is close to London. The Queen, moreover, can indulge her favourite pastime of riding in the private parklands and Prince Philip can play polo in Windsor Great Park.

Queen Elizabeth is the latest of an unbroken line of Kings and Queens who have contributed to more than eight centuries of history at Windsor. Samuel Pepys greeted this medieval stronghold as 'the most romantique castle .. in the world'. Certainly it is the world's oldest royal residence, but Windsor's sturdy walls do not encircle all its history. If the legend is true King Arthur and his knights sat round their famous Round Table in the neighbourhood of Windsor. What is unquestionable is that William the Conqueror, appreciating the strategic site close to the Thames, the main highway in those days, constructed one of his network of fortified strongpoints to suppress the hostile Saxons. To his heir William II (called Rufus) Windsor was no more than a fortress-prison, but his brother Henry I held Court there. From that time Windsor grew into a home for the Kings and Queens of England. But among this great sprawling mass the earliest surviving stonework dates from the reign of Henry II (1154–89), the first Plantagent, who replaced wood with stone. Today it merges into the royal apartments beside the east terrace.

Like Elizabeth II Henry I appears to have spent Christmas at Windsor. The *Anglo-Saxon Chronicle* reveals that during Christmas in 1126 the King compelled the Church hierarchy and the nobles 'to give England and Normandy after his death into the hand of his daughter Athelic (alias Maud or Mathilda)'.

The Christmas Court of Elizabeth II contrasts with that of her ancestor King John. For the King's festivity in 1213 the sheriffs in nearby counties were instructed to supply fifteen thousand herrings, three thousand capons, one thousand salted eels, four hundred pigs, a hundred pounds of fresh almonds, six thousand gallons of wine, and four casks of the finest wine for the sovereign's personal consumption.

John was besieged at Windsor in 1189, and it was from the castle that he left to fix his seal to Magna Carta in 1215 at Runnymede, a few miles downriver. Windsor has experienced some sombre moments and one of the darkest was in this monarch's reign. The King committed to one of the towers the wife and son of his former favourite, William de Braose, with merely a piece of raw bacon and a sheaf of wheat for food. Both were found dead eleven days later. 'Maud de Braose, in her last pangs of hunger, had gnawed the cheeks of her son, then probably dead, and after this effort she appeared to have fallen into the position in which she was found'.

Building programmes seem to have been an obsession of John's son, Henry III, who introduced a measure of comfort into the castle. It was Edward III, however, who injected some magnificence into the great gaunt castle and transformed it into a palace. Edward was born at Windsor where in January 1344 he had the romantic notion of reviving the Round Table and Arthurian idealism. Instead, four years later, he created the 'Most Noble and amiable Company of St George, named the Garter'. The story generally related of its origin, is that when the Countess of Salisbury dropped her blue garter Edward, possessed of 'a sparcle of fyne love that endured longe' picked it up and, putting it round his own leg, uttered the famous motto: 'Honi soit qui mal y pense'. To the sniggers of nearby courtiers he remarked, 'You make but small account of this garter, but within a few months I will cause the best of you all to reverence the like.' True or not the world's most famous order of chivalry was founded and each year Queen Elizabeth II and her Knights of the Garter meet in the perpendicular stone shrine of St George's Chapel (built by Edward IV who destroyed the first church) in June. Long ago Mass was said daily at Windsor for the Garter Knights. They were excused regular attendance and the reigning sovereign maintained 'Poor Knights ... decayed officers of gentle birth ... impotent of themselves or inclining to poverty' to represent them. To this day Windsor is the home of Military Knights who deputize at ceremonies in the absence of Garter Knights.

Down the years Kings and Queens have contributed to the story of Windsor. One can visualize, for instance, the obese figure of Henry VIII being hauled up the stairs by pulley and ropes because he was too grotesquely fat to climb them; his daughter Elizabeth who erected gallows outside the castle gate to dispose of anyone who arrived from London at a time of plague, and summoned Shakespeare to write the *Merry Wives of Windsor;* and the sad-faced Charles I, spending his last Christmas as a prisoner and, after his execution, being secretly buried in St George's.

Queen Anne delighted in the rural life of Windsor, spending much time there in her later and goutier days. After that the castle was neglected by the first two Georges. The third George intended to restore it, but it was his son George IV who completed the plan. With his usual extravagance he bestowed huge sums in knitting together the motley of buildings into the structure one can see today.

At first Queen Victoria was not particularly drawn to Windsor, but she became infected by Prince Albert's enthusiasm for rural life. In due course visits to the castle after the formality of Buckingham Palace were described as being 'freed from some dungeon'. It was at Windsor that she met and became engaged to Prince Albert. Windsor was also the sombre backcloth of his typhoid fever and the place where he died. From then onwards to Victoria Windsor was a shrine and to reside elsewhere on the anniversary of the Consort's death could never be contemplated.

Her great-great-granddaughter Elizabeth II has herself subscribed to changes at the castle down the years. On her instructions in 1960 the interior of the Edward III Tower was redesigned. As part of the rich panorama over eight centuries she decided that one suite should reflect her own age and engaged Sir Hugh and Lady Casson to present it in a modern key. The furniture, which was highly approved by the Furniture Makers' Guild, was greatly enhanced by the Queen's choice of twenty contemporary pictures.

Today Windsor Castle is not only the home of the House of Windsor but a vital facet of the household's economy. To reduce the cost in the royal homes, especially in the kitchens at Buckingham Palace, the royal gardens maintain a regular flow of flowers and vegetables. To meet the demands of staff and guests twenty-four acres are devoted solely to vegetables and a further eight acres are allotted to fruit. The area needed for flowers is about two acres; a slightly lesser area is under glass. The Queen has made it a rule that all vegetables must be pulled while they are young and tender. They are conveyed by van to Buckingham Palace each morning and cooked the same day.

When the Queen is on official duty in Scotland she lives in the Palace of Holyroodhouse. Here she resides for about a week each summer, which includes a royal garden party. Perhaps because of the Scottish element in her ancestry ancient ceremonies have been revived. When she mixes, for instance, with her Royal Company of Archers, wearing their attractive uniform, it is a return for a brief while to the glory of the past. Being so remote from London the Palace today is little used. Yet its history, replete with all the ingredients of venomous intrigue, brutal tragedy and romance, far outshines that of Buckingham Palace.

'Rood' is the medieval word for 'cross' and gave its name to this northern palace. A fascinating legend revealed by a fifteenth-century manuscript known as the *Holyrood Ordinale* relates how in 1128 David I, King of the Scots, ignored his confessor's advice not to hunt on the day of the Exaltation of the Holy Cross. He was wounded by a stag (which was the Devil in disguise), and as he seized the antlers the animal fled, and he found himself clutching a crucifix instead. During the night he dreamed that a voice ordered him 'to make a house for the Canons devoted to the Cross'. In consequence he founded the Augustinian Abbey of Holyrood. Another tale claims that Queen Margaret had the abbey built to accommodate a fragment of the True Cross. What is fact, however, is that a shrine arose and a road, known as Canongate, joined it with Edinburgh.

In medieval times Scottish Kings and Queens preferred the security of Edinburgh Castle about a mile away. But as assassination grew less probable they favoured the abbey guest house instead. James IV began to erect Holyroodhouse near by but made the error of quarrelling with his ebullient brother-in-law Henry VIII. As a result he died at Flodden Field. Building went on under his son James V, but in 1544, Henry, furious over the engagement of young Mary Queen of Scots to the French Dauphin (having decided she should become the bride of his son Edward) despatched the Earl of Hertford to 'sack Holyroodhouse'. However, much of the palace was left undamaged and when Mary, widowed by the death of Francis I of France, journeyed back to Edinburgh, Holyroodhouse was intact.

Mary Stuart Queen of Scots dominates the history of Holyroodhouse thanks to the melodrama, sinister intrigue and murder that pervaded her life. In 1565 she married Lord Darnley through whose treachery her Italian secretary David Rizzio was assassinated on 9 March the following year outside her bedchamber. Today an inscribed plate marks the place to which the body was dragged – the door of the audience chamber. After the fall of the Catholic Stuarts and the rise of Queen Elizabeth's Hanoverian ancestors Holyroodhouse was allowed to decay. Not until Queen Victoria and Prince Albert

L

visited Edinburgh in 1852 was the palace made fit for royal habitation.

Following a tradition begun by her great-great-grandmother Queen Elizabeth and her family spend their long summer holiday at Balmoral, near Braemar. Lying beside the silvery Dee and set against the silent loneliness of Lochnager Balmoral is not old like Holyroodhouse. When Queen Victoria first rented Balmoral House in 1848, it was so small that when the Prince Consort played billiards in one of the sitting rooms she had to move from chair to chair to make room for the players. A small bedroom was all that could be spared for the Cabinet member on duty. In 1852 Queen Victoria received an unexpected financial windfall : John Camden Nield, who has been described as an eccentric miser, bequeathed to her (without disclosing the reason) a quarter of a million pounds. Of this the Queen spent £31,500 in purchasing Balmoral and its 17,400 acres and then she had Albert replace the old house with an extensive granite baronial castle. As the laird of an estate Victoria resisted formality, mingling unostentatiously with the cottagers and ghillies. Exploring the enchanting countryside on ponies the royal pair travelled incognito as Lord and Lady Churchill, readily tolerating the vagaries of Highland weather and the primitive service of simple inns.

On this annual holiday on Deeside Queen Elizabeth carries on the tradition of royal laird. Here she can temporarily sever herself from formality, although she cannot ignore the official documents and other State business. For whether she is on vacation at Balmoral or Sandringham many of her household staff accompany her. The entourage is not as great as during the progresses of the first Elizabeth, for in earlier times the odds and ends of government, treasure, kitchen equipment and even the royal bed and chapel accompanied the itinerants. Nowadays, apart from the essential staff for the conduct of State affairs, the royal 'caravan' comprises little more than motorcars, horses, and dogs for the shooting. Speedy transport makes the Court extremely mobile, allowing the Queen's personnel to move quickly to and from London. The despatch boxes continue to arrive from the Ministries just as they followed the sovereign down the centuries, yet they travel more swiftly.

At Sandringham Elizabeth II is not only the Queen. Just as she is the laird at Balmoral she is also the squire on the Norfolk estate which Victoria's consort purchased out of the revenues of the Duchy of Cornwall for his son, the future Edward VII. The Prince began by remodelling the original house into a rambling red-brick mansion but became engrossed in the whole estate of six parishes. 'Sandringham improves in appearance every year', Edward wrote proudly to his mother. His new estate cottages were such model dwellings that the Liberal Government of the day invited him to sit on the Royal Commission on the Housing of the Working Class.

No doubt the jovial Edward VII would have displayed enthusiasm for his great-granddaughter's experiments at Sandringham. These are varied: from mushroom growing to carrot-washing machines and the preparation of frozen peas. Today the Queen is one of the country's foremost owners of thoroughbred (and prize-winning) cattle; for agriculture on a firm business footing figures large in the economy at Sandringham, an estate of some 20,000 acres, including some of Britain's most valuable land.

This leads to an intriguing question: how rich is the Queen? Clearly she is a person of great wealth. But is this to the degree that some people imagine? Wild rumours that the House of Windsor owns estate holdings in New York's Manhattan lack foundation. So too does speculation that huge family fortunes have been bequeathed from one generation to another (for the contents of royal wills are never made public). And although the Queen's treasures such as the old masters, the precious antiques, and the astonishing collection of porcelain are claimed to be worth some millions of pounds, it is inconceivable that she would ever dispose of them for personal gain. Take, for instance, the many paintings, valued at some

£50,000,000, a heritage reaching back to the time when Henry VIII engaged Hans Holbein as court painter. Free from the effects of death duties the pictures have accumulated over the centuries, so that it is now the only royal collection of such magnitude to exist. There are works by Rubens and Van Dyck, Canaletto and other Venetians. Michelangelo and Rembrandt are also amply represented and there are six hundred Leonardo da Vinci drawings alone.

Many treasures from a collection exceeding one thousand paintings were sold during Cromwell's Commonwealth. Some were regained after the Restoration but others – by Titian, Correggio and others – crossed to the continent for good. The existing pictures are bequeathed from monarch to heir. It is a gross error, therefore, to imagine that Queen Elizabeth could sell these works any more than she could attempt to dispose of the State-owned Crown Jewels. They are held for her successors. On view to the public at Hampton Court and Windsor Castle they have already cost the monarchy many thousands of pounds to maintain. To that extent it is arguable that they are a drain on the royal purse.

Although a good deal of the Queen's furniture was fashioned by those superb English craftsmen Robert Adam, Chippendale, Hepplewhite and Sheraton there is also a remarkable array of French eighteenth-century pieces (some of which came from the French royal palaces) acquired by George IV before and during the French Revolution, and at the conclusion of the Napoleonic Wars. Though a voluptuary the King had exquisite taste in furniture. In amassing these valuable items George was guided by an intimate, the third Marquis of Hertford, who introduced French furniture to the Wallace Collection in London. His French cooks Benois and Weltje were also invaluable as agents in Paris when furniture appeared in the sale rooms due to the Revolution. The sumptuous display of Sèvres porcelain – one of the most outstanding collections in the world – was also added to the British royal possessions about this time. And in the bow room at Buckingham Palace visitors stop to admire the most magnificent assemblage of English porcelain to be seen anywhere.

Intriguing too are the Queen's clocks. Altogether there are more than three hundred unusual timepieces at Buckingham Palace and some 360 at Windsor. Another 250 tick away the time at Balmoral and a further 160 at Sandringham. In this motley there are amazing clocks in gilt bronze and Chinese porcelain, grandfathers and pedestals, bracket clocks which chime, astronomical clocks and other rare horological specimens. One long-case clock occupied a place in the Palace of Versailles before the Revolution. Redolent of current joy and coming sadness is the silver-gilt timepiece replete with lovers knots which Henry VIII gave to the ill-fated Anne Boleyn on her wedding morning. Captivating for its uniqueness is the Negress Head clock bought by George IV. It is in gilt and patinated bronze, and the dusky maiden's fluttering eyelids tell the time; her left ear-ring operates a sixteen-pipe organ which plays eight different tunes.

A favourite hobby of the Queen's grandfather and father was collecting stamps – another inheritance worth more than a million pounds. Philately actually occupied George V three afternoons each week when State business permitted.

His granddaughter's pastime centres on horses, whether she is riding, breeding or racing them. George VI once jokingly said of his elder daughter, 'she's horse mad'. This love of horses was conspicuous even in childhood when, for instance, the little Princess (to the amusement of the Archbishop of Canterbury) led her grandfather on hands and knees by the beard; or when in the nursery, she tied the cords of her dressing-gown to the bedstead and drove imaginery horses. On the highest landing at Number 145 Piccadilly three dozen toy horses had to be groomed and fed. Lilibet had an affection for all kinds of horses: the hacks in Rotten Row, the heavy draught horses hauling the brewers' drays, the ponies drawing carts in London's streets. 'If I am ever Queen', she once remarked, 'I shall make a law that there must be no riding on Sundays. Horses should have rest.'

Childhood memories are often indelible. There is every likeli-
hood that King George V was the first to instil a love of horses
in his young granddaughter. When she was four it was from
her grandfather that she received her first pony, Peggy, a
Shetland. Within a year she was competent enough to ride a
short distance with the Pytchley: this was her father's gesture
to honour Frank Freeman, 'the finest huntsman of his time', on
his retirement, by having Lilibet enter the hunt. Today when
the Queen visits her racing stud at Sandringham, where stands
the massive statue of Persimmon, the Derby winner, she doubtless recalls the childhood tours of her grandfather. After lunch
on Sundays it was King George's practice to stroll round the
stables at Sandringham and Wolferton to see the mares and
yearlings.

In adult life the Queen has shown no penchant for hunting.
Neither has she any inclination to bet at race meetings. Her
cardinal interests are horsemanship and the breeding, training
and management of horses. These can be placed in two categories: those which she owns and trains at her expense at
Newmarket (and from which she takes all winnings); and the
horses bred by the National Stud and leased to the Queen
throughout their racing life (whose winnings are shared). Her
most celebrated horse was the chestnut Aureole which won
£36,225. When it went to stud at Sandringham it handsomely
helped to subsidize the Norfolk estate. In her first ten years as
an owner (perhaps her most successful period), the Queen's
stake winnings totalled more than £150,000.

The books in the Queen's study dealing with breeding and
racing convey her profound interest. She files a weekly racing
report, reads a racing newspaper whenever she can spare the
time, and has her own special index card system for breeding
bloodstock. The same enthusiasm was particularly marked in
her great-grandfather and grandfather. As in their case her
racing seasons have witnessed fluctuations of success and
failure. When she was thirteen she visited the stables at
Egerton House, Newmarket, there seeing on an archway a
panel bearing the stakes won by Edward VII. They look an

impressive record, yet all these victories inscribed in gilt have been eclipsed by the gains of his great-granddaughter.

For one who is so captivated by horses it is fitting that the Queen should possess her own racecourse. This is Royal Ascot – an extremely profitable source of income. Yet the Queen does not benefit financially, for the earnings are ploughed back into the course, stables and grandstand and already she has expended over a million pounds. This inheritance arose out of the impulsive whim of stout Queen Anne to whom the idea of sponsoring a race meeting came as she dashed across Ascot Heath during 1711. On a Saturday in August of that year horses raced for a plate, valued at £1,000, donated by Her Majesty. Royal Ascot thrived under subsequent monarchs, and William IV introduced the royal procession which the Queen and Prince Philip maintain each year.

To the Queen's treasures one can also add the most valuable personal collecion of jewellery, numbering some nine hundred items, in the world. But, again, would she be likely to dispense with any for financial gain?

Though information is singularly scanty it is more than probable that a wedding over six centuries ago led to the Queen's major source of private wealth. Through his marriage in 1359 to Blanche, heiress to the Duchy of Lancaster, John of Gaunt, fourth son of Edward III, acquired what might loosely be called the kernel of an estate, which totalled in due course some 52,000 acres. As Duke of Lancaster, John's son gained the Crown to rule as King Henry IV. That is why the Duchy came to be the personal holding of successive Kings and Queens. It is also why the choir in the Chapel of the Savoy sings 'God save the Queen ... bless our noble Duke'. Each year a City lawyer punctiliously weighs six horse shoes and sixty-one nails as a quit-rent relating to the site of a blacksmith's forge which once stood in the Strand. That was six centuries ago, but – like an echoing ring of the anvil – the rent has been paid annually ever since. This simple little ceremony signifies why the Queen (like her forbears) is said to receive ground rents from the

Savoy Hotel, the Savoy Theatre and a hotch-potch of shops and office blocks in the Strand and neighbouring Aldwych.

The Duchy of Lancaster is extensive, comprising not only London estates but large industrial areas in the north of England, the greater part of the spa at Harrogate and other prescriptive rights. All revenues – today more than £300,000 annually – enjoy exemption from income tax and death duties but, as in the case of her father, due to the erosive effects of inflation, the Queen has at times used part of her income to help pay for the institution of monarchy.

Beyond Buckingham Palace perhaps only a few trusted executives of Coutts and Co., who have been the royal bankers for more than two hundred years, are admitted to the secrets of the Queen's private resources. However, in a sense it is in character that a fourteenth-century legacy helps to sustain modern monarchy. For the institution of British monarchy is very old. It's antiquity is one of its cardinal assets. As Sir Ernest Barker once aptly wrote :

When a nation has preserved continuity with its past, and continues to feel some piety towards its past, it will naturally fly the flag of monarchy which it has inherited from its past. But the monarchy which it preserves will be a changing and moving monarchy – changing and moving with the times, and actively helping the times to change and move. That, for the last three hundred years, has been the nature of British monarchy. That is the secret of its survival, and that is the source of its strength.

♔ Select Bibliography

Sir Ivor Jennings, *The Queen's Government* (1954).

G. T. Warner and C. H. K. Marten, *The Groundwork of British History* (1923).

Walter Bagehot, *The English Constitution* (1867).

Dermot Morrah, *The Work of the Queen* (1958).

Allan A. Michie, *The Crown and the People* (1952).

Graham and Heather Fisher, *Elizabeth Queen and Mother* (1964).

James A. Frere, *The British Monarchy at Home* (1963).

HRH The Duke of Windsor, *The Crown and the People* (1953).

Helen Cathcart, *Her Majesty* (1962).

Geoffrey Wakeford, *Thirty Years a Queen* (1968).

Dorothy Laird, *How the Queen Reigns* (1959).

Helen Cathcart, *The Royal Bedside Book* (1969).

Dermot Morrah, *Princess Elizabeth* (1947).

Charles Mitchell, *The Queen's Horses* (1955).

Sir Harold Nicolson, *King George V* (1952)

❧ Index